"Having lost a child through miscarriage ourselves, we personally know the grief that can challenge a marriage and how that grief can be a stepping stone to the arms of Christ and his mother Mary. Watching our friends Ryan and Kelly Breaux's witness and their passion for walking with couples who have lost a child tells us that there is no doubt that they are living out their vocation to be balm to the souls of grieving parents. This book is like none other as it follows the heart of a grieving mother all the way to healing."

RYAN AND MARY-ROSE L. VERRET
Founder, Author, and Speaker
Witness to Love: Marriage Prep Renewal Ministry

"If ever there was a book that is a conduit of God's grace to those who need deep healing from grief, *Hiding in the Upper Room* is that book. Kelly, in her raw honest dialogue with God, shows how, through prayer and the sacraments, Christ can deliver you from the brink of despair to the peace that surpasses all understanding. This is a must read for anyone suffering trauma and loss."

SUSAN SKINNER
Catholic speaker, columnist, blogger, and Director
of Adult Faith Formation
St. Philip Catholic Church, Franklin, TN

Hiding

in the

Upper Room

HOW THE CATHOLIC SACRAMENTS HEALED ME
FROM THE GRIEF OF CHILD LOSS

KELLY BREAUX

Edited by Natalie Hanemann
nataliehanemann.com

Cover design by Kristen Ingebretson

CONTENTS

To my incredible husband Ryan, my beautiful daughter Estelle, my three little saints in heaven: Talon Antoine, Emma Grace, and Christian Ryan, and Jesus, my Savior. I love you so much!

FOREWORD

THE GOSPEL OF LUKE OPENS WITH AN EXPLANATION that Luke, "having followed all things closely," has decided "to compile a narrative of the things that have been accomplished" among them. As a disciple of St. Paul, St. Luke evangelizes the first century Jewish and Gentile worlds by writing his account of the Good News of the Divine Physician who comes "to proclaim good news to the poor, liberty to the captives, and recovery of sight to the blind, to set liberty to those who are oppressed, to proclaim the year of the Lord's favor" (Luke 4:18–19 quoting Isa. 61 and 58). St. Luke proclaims the truth that Jesus Christ heals, restores, liberates, forgives, and fulfills.

The Gospel of Luke ends and the Acts of the Apostles begins with the promise of the Holy Spirit who descends upon the Apostles and the Church. Christ does not abandon His Church as He promises in Matthew 28:20: "Behold, I am with you always, to the close of the age." Jesus Christ is still the Divine Physician. In this age of the Holy Spirit, He is still fulfilling the prophecy of Isaiah.

The Good News of who Jesus is and what He has done for us is recorded in the four Gospels of Sacred Scripture. Joining a multitude of Christians who have gone before them, in writing this book, Kelly and Ryan Breaux have written another page in the account of the Good News. Their candid testimony reveals how our Savior has brought liberty to the captivity of their grief, light to their darkness, and freedom from the oppression of their suffering.

I only met the Breaux's shortly after they began their journey back to a more authentic relationship with Jesus. Priests have a unique privilege of being able to closely witness Divine grace melt away the societal ill of the hard heart. "I will take away your heart of stone and give you a heart of flesh" (Ezek. 36:26). Watching Kelly's heart being melted by love for Christ and her community has been one of the most powerful displays of Divine power in our parish. Christ is alive. His Spirit is moving. Ryan and Kelly, even in sorrow, are bearing witness to these truths.

It has been said that a Christian is one who lives the life of Christ, or more intimately, is another Christ. Jesus gives the authentic invitation to Christian discipleship: "If anyone would come after me, let him deny himself and take up his cross and follow me" (Matt. 16:24). These words should pierce our hard hearts. Who is eager for ascetic self-denial or to carry the burden of crisis or even to be obedient to another? Even our Lord asked that the cup of suffering should pass from Him (cf. Matt. 26:39). It's a reasonable request. After all, only deranged people go out looking for pain. We know, though, that Jesus willingly endured His passion, took up His cross, and laid down His life. He did so to forgive us and save us from sin.

He did not suffer, however, to save us from suffering. He suffered to redeem suffering.

This side of heaven can be full of intense pain and soul-crippling sorrow. Kelly reveals her gut-wrenching encounter with this unbearable sorrow. She shows each of us, and some of you may well sympathize, the pain of her cross. We see her pain, bitterness, anger, despair, and brokenness—all symptoms of the burden of the cross. Suffering is real and it's ugly and it's very human. This is not only the story of a mother's grief, however. Kelly shows us the depth of her pain so we may know the heights of Christ's healing power. Immense power comes down from heaven through the sacraments. Kelly and Ryan testify to the power of Christ truly present in each of His sacraments.

The God of Jesus Christ is the God of healing, precisely because He knows suffering. "We do not have a high priest who is unable to sympathize with our weaknesses" (Heb. 4:15). He invites us to take up our crosses and follow Him because He has an answer for the cross. Only Jesus can say, "Come to me all who labor and are heavy laden, and I will give you rest" (Matt. 11:28). Jesus' mutilated dead body did not remain in the tomb, it resurrected!

There is something about suffering that can lead to glory. Suffering, and healing from suffering, can be an intimate encounter with the Divine Physician. It can bring about greater empathy and a genuine wisdom. There is wisdom in the cross. It shows us the virtuous way of suffering with patience and the deep human connection of vulnerability. Ultimately, though, the cross shows us that suffering is rooted in love. The pain of loss is born from love of the lost. There is something very human and raw, but also very beautiful about this.

Grief is the willingness to suffer personal pain out of love for another. While I believe Jesus grieves with us in our pain, it is not where He wants us to remain.

Kelly has shared her story of victory she and Ryan have found in Christ. Their grief, rooted in love, has been transformed into union with the wounded hearts of Jesus and Mary. Christ has invigorated them to love passionately and to live authentically. Kelly writes with profound depth of her love for Jesus whom she has come to know personally through the sacraments of His Church. It is this same Jesus who has brought salvation to her children and restoration to her life. Her story is one of an ordinary Christian, carrying extraordinary pain, who has allowed Christ, the Divine Physician, to offer her the saving remedy of His mercy, tenderness, and compassion.

This medicine is offered to all who seek it in faith. I am grateful that Kelly and Ryan have answered the call the share this story so all may know the power of Jesus Christ who comes to save us and set us free.

REV. GARRETT MCINTYRE
Pastor, St. Bernard Catholic Church
Breaux Bridge, Louisiana

But he said to me, "My grace is sufficient for you, for my power is made perfect in weakness." I will all the more gladly boast of my weaknesses, that the power of Christ may rest upon me.

—2 Corinthians 12:9

Introduction

I'M JUST ME

"And he said, 'Hear my words: If there is a prophet
among you, I the LORD make myself known to him
in a vision, I speak with him in a dream.'"

—Numbers 12:6

I AM AN ORDINARY MOM OF FOUR CHILDREN, ONE ON
earth and three in heaven, who was given an extraordinary cross to
carry called "Child Loss." Usually that statement stops people in
their tracks, but I think most of you who have picked up this book
want to know more about healing from child loss or else help someone who is suffering through it. For this, I commend your courage,
brave warrior.

My husband Ryan and I have been married for seventeen years.
Over the years, our marriage has suffered more loss than most
ever will, and while the grief has been overwhelming at times, it
was through these losses that I found my way back to the Catholic
Church and back to myself. Our story may be hard to read and di-

gest, but hold on to the end, there is hope and healing. It is possible for you too.

When I was a little girl, I dreamed of one day getting married and having two children, a boy and a girl. I imagined we would live in a white house with a large yard surrounded by a white picket fence, and a dog leaping around our heels. I dreamed of having a good life. But it was only a dream. My reality looks a good bit different than that.

My idea of a good life was a fairy-tale. It was shaped by sit-coms, and magazine articles with titles like "How to Be Happy" and "You'll Be Successful If . . ." These were ideals that I held as goals for my life, my path to finding happiness. With hard-fought knowledge, I have learned that happiness is a feeling that usually is not what people are truly searching for. Most people would say what they desire more than anything is peace.

Growing up, I wasn't taught how to deal with the real hardships of life. So it came as a shock that I was facing life-and-death situations at only twenty-five years old. I had not been raised in the Catholic faith, so I had never heard of redemptive suffering. In my Christian infancy, I believed Christ died for our sins so that we would be happy and never suffer. After watching both of my children die in front of me, I knew that would not be my story. Happiness would never be possible for me. How do you survive child loss? That is an honest question I asked myself often.

I hate to use the cliché "It takes time" but for me, that was true. By the grace of God, the Lord did not leave me in my misery. He stayed with me, even when I resisted, and eventually, He brought me out of it. This took many years, and I had to relearn how to trust and to love as though I were learning to speak a new language.

My healing began with a dream. While at the deepest points of my grief, I demanded God give me a reason for allowing Ryan and me to endure the unthinkable. I needed to hear from God something . . . anything! . . . that would help us process the hurt we felt trapped in.

I asked the question "Why?" more times than I've asked any question before. I joke that God probably was tired of hearing me ask it so often, and so He answered just to shut me up. I said God gave me His response in a dream, but actually, God spoke to me over the course of several dreams. He didn't offer a sufficient response to my pleadings, but what He did was help me to understand how He has been present in my life from the beginning. I discovered that *His* will for my life and *my* will for my life were not the same. In spite of this, His love for me ran deeper than I could fathom. His love conquered my spiritual death.

These dreams helped me see past my grief, which had been mystically clouding my vision for a long time. My grief was suffocating me and wouldn't allow my broken heart to heal.

The idea for this book began after waking up from one particular dream. In this dream, the Lord answered the question I'd been asking Him over and over since my daughter Emma's death. *Why? Why, Lord, did You forget me? Why did You skip me in the mercy line? Why did You not heal my babies? Why did You not raise them from the dead? Why didn't You take me instead?*

In my dream, I saw God, I heard His voice, I felt His warmth, I sensed His Love and His mercy at the same time. God spoke in a gentle, confident voice. *"What if I had come to you and told you—before you had conceived—that you would have not one baby, but two—a son named Talon and a daughter named Emma Grace—and they would be twins. What if I'd told you they were not yours to keep, but a gift?"* He stretched out His arms, which held my two babies and said, *"Behold your gifts."* He paused for a long moment, then said, *"But you will only have Talon for fifteen days, and you'll only have Emma Grace for three years, ten months, and twenty-five days. Would you have said, then, what you are saying now? Do you still want your precious gifts? Do you want your twins?"*

As I looked at God with my devastated heart, my answer was and always will be *"Yes, Lord, I want my gifts,"* because that is what they were. Talon and Emma were given to Ryan and me for a reason: to love and to learn from. This yes was my fiat, when I said to the Lord, *"Let it be done according to Thy Word."* Though, like Mary, saying yes would come with incredible pain.

I questioned God further. *"But they weren't here long enough. Lord, I know they were borrowed from You, but I want them back."* I begged Him to give me understanding, but He looked at me with the love only He can give and said, *"They were only gifts to you. Gifts for you to treasure and love, but only for a time."* And for the first time since their deaths, I began to understand. Their purpose on earth was complete, and they had returned to the Father, to eternity.

This was a turning point in my healing process. I never thought God would give me an option, to either go through this unbearable suffering or to have never known my twins at all. But in this dream, it seemed to me that He was leaving the decision up to me, because He waited for me to respond. My head understood why God had allowed these beautiful gifts to have been given, then taken, but my heart wasn't ready yet. If I'm being honest, my heart is still not fully ready just yet. My head and my heart do not function in sync, and they battle each other for victory.

God was telling me that to move forward in the grieving process, I needed to accept that the twins were not ours but His. But how could I accept this? I didn't know if I could ever trust Him again. I had given Him my heart and it felt like He hadn't fully accepted my gift. Why now? Why pray? Why trust? My heart, which at the time was fragile as the bones of a baby bird, could not bear it.

I didn't want to admit I was not okay with God taking the twins back. Because I thought that if I admitted this, I would be a "bad" Catholic. My pride did not allow me to fully submit. I wanted to keep them with me, to raise them into adulthood, to enjoy their lives for the rest of my life, but this wasn't God's plan. As painful as it has been to accept, over time, it has become my reality. I knew that surrendering was my only option for healing. It was in my surrender that I truly understood His love for me and for the twins.

Waking from the dream, I knew immediately that God had given me another gift: the ability to understand how much He still loves me. Jesus laid the request on my heart, in silence, but etched in stone. *Write it down, and start your book.*

Let me say upfront, I am not a writer. I don't even think I made a C in college English. I don't have a good handle on grammar or verb tenses. God's request scared me, but I wanted to be obedient to Him. So I began to write.

It quickly became evident that God didn't intend for me to write the entire book at that exact point in my grief journey. This confused me at first, because why would He ask me to do something and not give me the tools to accomplish it? God stopped me that day because He was not finished forming me yet for this mission.

I needed to gain some perspective. I needed the emotional room to have empathy for others and not be so focused on myself. It has taken me a long time to process those difficult years. More than ever, the ability, in humility, to give my all to Him and admit I couldn't do it alone. God had to be gentle and patient with me as my big heart gets hurt easily. I'll admit, for a long time, I was like a Fabergé egg. As time passed, though, new words started to bubble up from inside me again, until one day I sat down and was able to finish the story.

How does He do this? How does He fill a hollow shell? I felt mystified by what was happening to my heart and soul because I didn't think healing was possible for me. I'd had this thought for so long, I had started to believe it.

The words contained in this book are what Jesus laid on my heart; words that are so obviously not from me; they contain a wisdom that I clearly do not possess. I am no theologian, I do not have a psychology degree—I haven't even finished college . . . I'm just me. But what the world needs more of is witnesses, not theologians. I hope to be a witness of just how much Christ loves you, and for you to know that I am not qualified for this mission He has given me. But He has confirmed this mission time and time again. God does not call the qualified, He qualifies the called. This book is another example of what God accomplished by the lowliest of servants, fully willing but only partially knowing.

It took time for me to understand *why* God asked me to write down my story. Time passed. So many words were written, and yet the book still didn't have a name. Then, while sitting at a Mother's Day reflection at our diocese in 2018, God gave me direction through the following verse:

> On the evening of that day, the first day of the week, the doors being shut where the disciples were, for fear of the Jews, Jesus came and stood among them and said to them, "Peace be with you." When he had said this, he showed them his hands and his side. Then the disciples were glad when they saw the Lord.
>
> —John 20:19–20a

A friend shared with me her interpretation of this verse. She told me, "When Jesus said, 'Peace be with you' and showed the disciples His wounds, He was inviting us to show Him our wounds as well."

God was revealing to me a way to describe what I had done for so many years. These were the words that I was looking for to share this story. The phrase "Peace be with you" invited me to show my wounds to everyone. Because for so long, I shielded my wounds for fear of how uncomfortable they made me—and others—feel. It wasn't that I was hiding them from select people; I was hiding them from everyone. I wore a mask and few were aware of the depths of my pain.

Jesus spoke these words to His disciples when they were hiding in the Upper Room after the resurrection. They had locked the doors. Today we lock everything because of the world we live in, but in Jesus' time, doors were not typically locked, so this detail is significant. The disciples were afraid because the followers of Christ were being persecuted by the Romans. They hid from the Romans because of their human weakness. Like that door, my heart, too, was locked because I was afraid of what would happen if it opened.

Jesus knew the disciples would be afraid when He appeared, so He first offered them His peace and then showed them His wounds. It was an invitation from Christ for the disciples to give Him their own wounds. Christ's followers were broken, confused, angry, grief-stricken, and bitter. These emotions are typical when going through the trauma of losing a loved one.

Locking people out is exactly what I'd been doing for so long. Like Naomi in the Book of Ruth, I tried to push all the Ruths out of my life. Everything that was wrong with my relationship with Christ—my marriage, my vocation as a mother, my friendships—revolved around me hiding my grief and pushing people away.

When people endure this level of pain, they don't tend to share it. It's not pretty. Often when they look back on a time when they had shared it, they are shocked at the emotions and reactions they displayed while in the darkest of trenches. People aren't comfortable here. I am confirmation that people's nightmares do exist.

My story makes people aware that child loss isn't something that happens elsewhere, and that scares them. I tended to stuff my pain deep down to protect other people from feeling uncomfortable. But let it be known that if a person does not go up to meet this giant called grief, he will come down to meet them. Our grief will keep coming closer and closer, trying to consume us.

Society loves to paint perfect pictures of perfect lives. Open any of the social media sites and you'll see posts with beautiful, flawless people. This may elicit feelings of joy or contentment for some, but for a lot of us, seeing perfect lives brings up feelings of jealously and envy. We all want a perfect life, but perfect does not exist.

People run from suffering. We may think of suffering children in other countries and feel a remote compassion, but when it's close to home, or in our home, it forces us to react. It seems our culture would prefer to maintain a distance. One reason society protects itself from experiencing pain and suffering could be that it distorts their idea of beauty. By sharing images of perfection—be it a child, a house, or a body—it creates a false sense of what success looks like and how relationships are supposed to function. The truth is, we are all far from perfect. Thankfully, that is not what God is asking of us. He is asking us to be holy, not perfect.

If we feed ourselves on society's ideals, we are consuming only half-truths. We are all broken in some way. Our brokenness doesn't mean we are weak. On the contrary, I believe it glorifies God. It's in the broken that we see beauty, like the pieces that make up a stained-glass window, or in the bread broken in the Eucharist, or in the crushing of grapes to make wine.

We need to recognize what true beauty and true love looks like, because it does not come in the shape of a diamond; it comes in the shape of a cross. A cross many of us are unwilling to kiss.

The love story between me and my husband is not the kind depicted in music or on the movie screen. Love comes in the form of showing compassion for the weak and vulnerable. Beauty and love are shown through sacrifice. Jesus showed us what sacrificial love looks like, and He is the only one who can heal our deepest wounds.

He takes us, broken and in pieces, like stained glass, and transforms us into something beautiful.

It wasn't until I realized my true interior beauty that I was able to understand my mission. Through my losses I realized where God was calling me. He was calling me into battle like He had called David to fight Goliath. He was asking me to find my five smooth stones and to slay my giant. To face him in the trenches, in the valley of the shadow of death, to come in the name of the Lord, to sling my stones, and end his life. My grief was my giant.

It was in giving back to God the gift of my children that I came to understand what parents who are experiencing child loss go through during the healing process. I cannot convey the depth of my sympathy for anyone grieving the loss of a loved one. My heart cracks wide open in agony when I hear of a mother and father losing their child. I want to take that pain away from them, but I know I can't.

There is a common saying that parents of child loss belong to a club of ugly shoe-wearers, shoes no one wants to wear. Only those who have experienced child loss know how to walk in ugly shoes. I want to walk alongside you, wearing my own ugly shoes. And help you wear your own ugly shoes, to face your grief.

Only Jesus can heal you. But I wrote this book so I could share in carrying your cross like Simon of Cyrene helped Jesus to carry His. I want to help you identify what your five stones look like.

I came across this short vignette and it illustrates what I hope to do in sharing my story and offering comfort to those who grieve.

The Starfish Story

original story by Loren Eisley

One day a man was walking along the beach when he noticed a boy picking something up and gently throwing it into the ocean. Approaching the boy, he asked, "What are you doing?" The youth replied, "Throwing starfish back into the ocean. The surf is up and the tide is going out. If I don't throw them back, they'll die." "Son," the man said, "don't you realize there are miles and miles of beach and hundreds of starfish? You can't make a difference!"

After listening politely, the boy bent down, picked up another starfish, and threw it back into the surf. Then, smiling at the man, he said . . . "I made a difference for that one."[1]

My mission is to help you find what took me years. For this book to be effective, it requires that I be vulnerable and share my grief, my struggles, and my walk through the journey of healing, which has not yet ended. I have to remind myself of what my five stones are, so that when my giant tries to revive himself, I can quickly defeat him again.

I am someone who prefers to grieve privately. I'm uncomfortable crying in front of people. Holding in my tears so I don't ugly cry is

---

[1] Eisley, Loren. "The Star Thrower" published in *The Unexpected Universe* by Harvest (1972).

an effort. Grief takes work. But it is possible. In this book, I take off my mask and look at the monster called "grief."

My story may seem tragic if you only look at the deaths of my children and not at the blessings God has given me. Early in my grief journey, I had a hard time carrying my own cross. I felt ashamed and weak, and I was unwilling to surrender myself to God. But I found a source of truth and started to visualize my own resurrection. I found healing in the sacraments of the Catholic Church. This is my truth. The source of the light that now consumes my dark.

Writing this book has been difficult, but I can't help you if I don't tell you my story. I write about the many times our family was given horrifying news. Healing took me years . . . years to empty myself of my pride, my selfishness, my control, my envy and jealousy, my suffering, my vanity, my lack of trust, my fear, my OCD . . . I had to take out all my garbage before I could let Jesus "under my roof" to heal my heart.

Jesus revealed to me my purpose, and His plan for me. And for some reason, dear reader, he wrote your name down for me to touch as well. There is no coincidence that you are reading this book and experiencing this information at this point in your story. In hindsight, I can see that God had my hand every step of this journey. He has yours too. Just look down and meditate on that for a while.

Just as it is with Christ's passion and resurrection, you have to know the story to be able to honestly look at the cross and enter into His suffering. This is the only way our hearts can unite with Christ.

This is my story . . .

Part One

MY WORLD TRANSFORMED IN FRONT OF ME

"Fear not, little flock; for it is your Father's good pleasure to give you the kingdom."

—Luke 12:32, KJV

Chapter One

LOVE IN THE SHAPE OF A CROSS

"There is no fear in love, but perfect love casts out fear. For fear has to do with punishment, and he who fears is not perfected in love. We love, because he first loved us."

—1 John 4:18–19

I CAN REMEMBER THE FIRST TIME I SAW HIS FACE. I was eighteen years old, living on my own, and attending the University of Southern Louisiana for Interior Decorating. I was on Christmas break and a friend and I had gone to a bar in Lafayette to scope out the boys, dance, and have some fun.

We were walking back from the restroom toward the dance floor when she spotted this guy she knew, so we stopped to say hi. He had a friend standing next to him who was so good-looking, I couldn't stop staring. I felt giddy inside. He seemed mature and respectful—different from the guys my age who usually frequented this bar. He introduced himself to me using a fake last name, something I later learned, because he was seeing someone else and shouldn't have been talking to me even in passing. I laugh at this now because I'll need to have this conversation with our daughter one day about dating guys with wandering eyes.

I guess he and this girlfriend weren't that serious because he chatted with me for a couple minutes. Lucky for me, that wasn't the last time he came to this bar, and over the course of two months, I found myself looking for him each time my friends and I went. Silly, innocent, teenaged infatuation.

Then the day came when the thoughts of that cute boy speaking to me again became a reality. On Mardi Gras day of 1999, just two weeks before my nineteenth birthday, he walked up to me and seemed to be a totally different person, confident and flirty. He and his girlfriend had broken up. Ironic or divine, I consider it was providence that his previous relationship hadn't worked out.

From that day forward, we were inseparable. He was a perfect gentleman and swept me off my feet. I knew after two weeks that I wanted to marry him. He was kind and gentle, and he had this deep peace about him that was a mystery to me. But I eventually figured it out, as week after week, I hopped into his truck to attend Mass with him.

All of my friends had been raised Catholic, which was not uncommon in southern Louisiana where Acadian culture and Catholicism go hand in hand. I didn't understand the teachings of the Catholic Church because my mother had left her Catholic roots when I was still a young girl. But I had a deep curiosity about that faith tradition even before I met Ryan. While in school at USL, on days when life wasn't going great, I'd sneak into a back pew of Our Lady of

Wisdom Catholic Church on campus and pray. Sometimes, I would sit through a Mass, but more often I would go when the sanctuary was empty and I could just be with Jesus.

There was something profoundly different inside a Catholic Church that, at the time, I couldn't put my finger on, but when I sat down or knelt to pray, I felt that Jesus was present with me. I know now what that feeling was: the Real Presence of the body and blood of Christ in the Eucharist inside the tabernacle, something that can only be found within a Catholic Church.

Dating Ryan was the best decision I'd made up to that point in my life. Another piece of advice I'll give my daughter in a few years is to always date someone you can picture spending the rest of your life with. I could see what our life together would look like. Ryan was one of those guys who set the bar high for me. He was not only good-looking, he was charismatic and could make me laugh even when I was angry. He was kind and considerate. He was very selfless, a quality that I didn't even realize that I needed.

We went everywhere together, and our relationship was a mix of friendship and love. It is a gift in a marriage to be able to laugh with your best friend and soulmate. Ryan has a heart of gold and always has my best interest at heart. The love he has for our family leaves me in awe. Often, it's the women who have the larger presence in church, for whatever the reason. But for the first time, in Ryan, I saw a man who loved God—something I hadn't seen much growing up. My mother was the one who took me to church and taught me about God. I understand now how important it was to have a husband who has a strong faith life.

I often laugh that poor Ryan gets volunteered to volunteer by his wife—or we laugh that he is "volun-told"—but he does it with a smile. He has a charitable heart, always has a smile on his face, and is ready to lend a helping hand to anyone in need. This is the man that I married, and through each bump in the road, I'm always proud that I have him by my side—my rock, a warrior for Christ. My mother would always tell me her prayers had been answered because she couldn't have picked better spouses for me and my sister. I am blessed, I am loved, and I am so grateful.

Ryan and I dated for three years before he proposed. We met with Father Breaux—Ryan's ancestors founded the town, so the name is popular here—and attended the one-day engaged encounter where the Church shares with couples all of the Church teachings regarding the sacrament of marriage. It's impossible to cover everything a person needs to grow in their faith and prepare for such a monumental sacrament, the vocation of their adult life.

On July 13, 2002, before we said "I do" at our home parish of St. Bernard Church in Breaux Bridge, Louisiana, Ryan went to confession, but I did not. No one had explained to me how important this was, and when I found out Ryan had gone, I felt betrayed. If it had been important for him, why hadn't anyone told me that I should go? I should have been given the opportunity to enter this marriage in sanctifying grace, and I was brokenhearted to find out years later that I'd missed the opportunity. To be fair, it's likely they assumed I already knew.

Our wedding day was the best day of my life, up to that point. I walked down the aisle to the man of my dreams, and we said our vows before Christ in front of our friends, family, and God, not knowing what kind of life we were going to have. I had no idea what marriage would be like, but I knew I did not want it to be anything like my parents' marriage. It was important to me to remain married to this man who I loved dearly. At a marriage conference recently, one of the speakers described divorce as taking the cross off our marriage and placing it on the children.

Ryan and I committed that day, divorce would never be an option.

Chapter Two

RYAN'S ACCIDENT

> "Which is easier, to say to the paralytic, 'Your sins are forgiven,' or to say, 'Rise, take up your pallet and walk'?"
>
> —Mark 2:9

SEVEN MONTHS AFTER THE WEDDING, RYAN AND I left for a weekend of dirt-bike racing in Texas. We planned to attend the Houston Super Cross on Saturday night, and Ryan was going to enter the Sunday races at the outdoor track in Splendora. On Sunday, Ryan's bike was acting up so he decided to use a friend's bike in the race. Even though he wasn't familiar with this borrowed bike, he was very familiar with the sport.

For some reason that I still cannot comprehend today, they combined the pro-class with the intermediate class. Ryan was an intermediate rider. They lined up each group separately, and Ryan got the hole shot off the gate, which means he was in first place at the first corner. Then midway through the track, they started the pro-class racers.

While making the second lap, the guy in the lead for the pro-class fell and the rest of the pro-class passed him, along with some of the intermediate class. The guy who fell was racing for money, so he got up and made like a bandit to catch the rest of the pack. When he caught up with Ryan, the guy charged the jump at the same time as Ryan. Ryan gave him too much room, which he didn't realize until it was too late. Instead of Ryan's bike landing on the tabletop, he landed on a 55-gallon drum that projected him forty feet into the air. He landed on his head, shattering the paint on his helmet.

I had been filming the race from on top of our camper, so when he fell, I dropped the video camera and ran to him. It took me a while to get to him because of my location, so a crowd had surrounded him when I finally arrived. The breath had been knocked out of him, and in-between breaths, he was screaming in agony. No matter how hard he tried, he couldn't seem to catch his breath. I was trying to comfort him from a short distance, but I was having a hard time catching my own breath. Shock was setting in quickly.

I can remember his dad telling him he was okay, while Ryan was walking and struggling to deal with the pain in his back. Ryan had raced for a long time and so had his father. He had fallen many, many times before, but this time seemed more serious. He was grabbing his chest and his back, literally groaning in pain. Ryan's dad was trying to diffuse the fear, but I demanded he be taken to the hospital. Ryan agreed to get on the golf cart, and they drove him to the ambulance.

As we approached the ambulance, Ryan tried to adjust himself to get off the golf cart, and as he went to shift his weight to rise, he realized he was paralyzed from the waist down. Panic overcame us, and we all began to cry. I watched the paramedics physically lift him, as carefully as they could, and strap him to the board. My whole body went numb, and rapid-fire thoughts bounced around my head like hail on a tin roof. I knew the sport was dangerous, but never did I imagine Ryan could be severely injured. I climbed inside the ambulance and prayed as I held his hand, begging God to heal him.

Ryan was taken to the hospital in Splendora, Texas where they ordered an MRI of his spine. The hospital was not equipped for trauma, so when the doctor read the report that indicated a severe injury, the hospital called AirMed immediately to begin their route to the hospital. Ryan had broken his back and needed emergency surgery. I remember clearly, when we were in the hospital room by ourselves, Ryan muttering, "Please don't leave me if I'm paralyzed." I told him to stop saying that, but it was clear my sweet husband was afraid that I would abandon him. Ryan hung on his own cross that day, alone, humiliated, and afraid.

When the helicopter landed to retrieve Ryan, I looked inside before stepping in and realized there was no room for me to travel with him. My panic level skyrocketed. Ryan would have to be at the hospital alone for more than an hour while we drove. I began having a severe panic attack, struggling to catch my breath. No one should be left alone when they are injured and frightened. A man needs his wife and family with him.

As they prepared him for the transport to Houston, Ryan asked me again, over the noise of the whirling blade, if I would divorce him if he was paralyzed. I could only comfort him with a kiss as we said our goodbyes, both crying hard as the door closed.

As I'm typing this, Ryan and I will soon celebrate seventeen years of marriage. At the time, I brushed off his concern that I may not stay with him, but it makes me realize something poignant. We had so many chances to give up on each other over the years, but we love each other so much. Ryan and I rarely argued about anything of substance. We were stupid-crazy in love, googly-eyed, no one else in the room when we were having a conversation. Yes, we are that couple, but we've been handed lemons so many times in our married life. And each time, we always chose to make lemonade, because we truly loved each other. We sacrificed and chose love at every turn.

It wasn't easy, none of this has been easy—in fact, it's the exact opposite. I can only thank Jesus for allowing us to remain married, because I know it was Him who gave us the strength to keep fighting. It was Him who provided the daily grace. It was Him who revealed to us what marriage is supposed to look and feel like. He showed us the way to not only survive, but to thrive intimately with each other. Marriage is sacred and forever. "Therefore what God has joined together, let no one separate" (Mark 10:9, NRSVCE).

Ryan's surgery that night lasted eight hours. The entire time, I prayed for a miracle. I prayed for a blessing that my husband would be able to walk again. When the doctor entered the waiting room hours later, the only thing he could tell us was that the surgery had gone well, and from what he could see, Ryan had all range of motion. The Lord had blessed Ryan with a miracle. Our prayers had been heard and answered. Soon after, the love of my life was able to walk.

That accident should have left Ryan paralyzed from the waist down or possibly even from the neck down. In fact, his surgeon does a case study for medical students who are in their final years of orthopedic surgery training, and each year he presents Ryan's case. Most of the students raise their hands when the surgeon asks them if they think this patient remained paralyzed. No one knows how the spinal cord moved millimeters and not one single fragmented piece touched the spinal cord. His T3 and T5 compressed, cracked, and then shattered and dislodged his T4 vertebrae. The simple fact that nothing was touched was proof that God and His angels had intervened.

I know it was God who saved him and restored his ability to walk, something we take for granted every day. Rolling out of bed each morning and walking to the bathroom to get dressed is a gift from God. Ryan was given a second chance to experience playing kick ball with his daughter Estelle, and will one day have the privilege of walking her down the aisle. There is always something we can be grateful for in the midst of our suffering.

Ryan was in STICU for several days and then placed in a regular room for about a week. We were blessed, but not without suffering. It was the start of a difficult time for us. Two weeks before Ryan's accident, I had been let go from my job after a three-month trial period. I was devastated that I hadn't measured up to my manager's expectations, but the blessing of being able to care for Ryan at home and not worrying about work responsibilities relieved some of my anxieties.

However, not working comes with its own set of anxieties. Neither Ryan nor I could work for some time after his accident. He could barely walk and needed help transitioning from place to place, and so I became his nurse, caring for him 24/7. We went from two full incomes to one income that was paying two-thirds of his salary. We tried to stay focused on the fact that Ryan's life was spared; that was enough to keep us smiling.

Every couple of weeks we would make the trip to his surgeon in Houston. The car ride was excruciating for him. I watched as he gritted his teeth in agony. Ryan is a level-headed person and adamant about not getting addicted to pain medication, so he abruptly stopped taking it after a few weeks. As a result, every move was uncomfortable for him. To this day, he has times when he would benefit from pain medicine, but he flushed the remaining supply down the toilet soon after the surgery and won't get a new prescription. His fortitude inspires me.

Ryan stayed out of work for a total of six months. He was finally given the green light to return to work after gaining clearance from his physician and physical therapist. I don't think I've ever seen anyone so excited to go back to work, but Ryan's smile gleamed ear to ear that first morning back. Who actually loves to work? My husband, of course.

What a blessing that he could go back to work after having such a severe injury. Many people are disabled for the rest of their lives and become a prisoner to their pain, or they require permanent medication for chronic pain, go to multiple doctor appointments, and contend with deteriorated mobility. Although Ryan can't do everything he did before, he is able to do much more than we ever imagined.

What would have been easier for God to say to Ryan during this trial? "Your sins are forgiven" or grant the prayer request and say, "Arise and walk"?

God spoke to us on that day, but it did not radically transform our hearts. Not yet.

Chapter Three

KELLY'S PRAYER

"In her deep anguish Hannah prayed to the LORD, weeping bitterly. And she made a vow, saying, 'LORD Almighty, if you will only look on your servant's misery and remember me, and not forget your servant but give her a son, then I will give him to the LORD for all the days of his life.'"

—1 Samuel 1:10–11, NIV

AFTER RYAN RECOVERED AND WE BOTH RETURNED to work, we were ready to start a family. By this time, we had been married a little over a year and our love had only intensified as he healed from his accident. Our savings account was depleted from the medical bills and lack of steady income, but we desired to have a baby and began trying.

For the first few months, getting pregnant was just an idea, but then as month after month passed, it became evident that I wasn't getting pregnant. Sadness and anxiety began growing in my heart.

One day, I realized we had been trying to conceive for *eighteen months*! The reality hit us: we might have an issue with our fertility.

I think most women assume they'll be able to get pregnant with no problems. For the first time, I considered that I may not be one of those women. As the shock of that reality set in, Ryan and I decided it was time to see a fertility specialist.

We did not know at the time that we should have consulted with our priest to understand Church teaching on fertility. We trusted in God, but it never occurred to us that getting fertility treatments was taking the role of determining when life begins and ends away from God and putting it into our own hands.

If you are in the painful place of not being able to conceive on your own, I encourage you to seek guidance from your priest. Not only will your priest explain the Church's stance on IVF, but he can put you in contact with Natural Family Planning teachers. NFP helps a woman understand when her body is most and least likely to conceive. This is a safe and non-toxic path that helps you plan your family using and respecting God's design of the female body.

Consulting with your priest when facing infertility also provides you with another prayer partner and support system for you and your spouse. If we had discussed our situation with our priest, he would have gladly offered up Masses and prayers for us. We needed so many prayers during these days—for our child, for our marriage, and for our sanity. We needed to know God still loved us and that our church family was praying for our future baby. It would have been an incredible blessing to us.

Meanwhile, the part of my heart that was made to mother burned with the desire to hold my child. During this time, I would start off my morning asking God to send me a baby, and each night I would close my eyes and dream of a time when we would hold our own sweet child. I begged God to spare me this pain and bless us with a child, but the more time that passed, the deeper my prayers went and, in hindsight, I can see trying to get pregnant was becoming an obsession.

I never considered our infertility could be hereditary, but I learned my mother had trouble getting pregnant with me. All my life I'd thought it was just a coincidence that my sister and I are almost nine years apart. My sister also had trouble getting pregnant with my godson Konnor, and then also with my niece Kaylen. And there I was experiencing it myself.

We did simple screenings to see if my body was in good working order. These tests made me feel like a science project. "Stick here, take this, try that, lay on this side, lay on the other side, on this day do this, then the next day . . ." It was making my head spin. In the end, they found no evidence that anything was physically wrong with me. Getting us pregnant was to be a process of trial and error.

The first medicine my doctor prescribed was Clomid, a drug used to prevent symptoms of PCOS (Polycystic Ovarian Syndrome). I was never diagnosed with PCOS but my doctor prescribed it in the hopes that it would help with ovulation. After several days with no positive response, my doctor told me my ovaries evidently thought Clomid was candy, as they had not responded.

The next step was a little more invasive: fertility shots every morning and evening on certain days, and then an HCG (Human chorionic gonadotropin) shot on a specific day to trigger the release of my egg. This was harder for my body to tolerate. It wasn't a cake-walk for my marriage either.

The roller coaster of hormones created lots of emotional highs and lows—sad one day, happy the next, sad and happy in one day, and then sad and happy in the same moment. The ups and downs were hard on me and Ryan and on some days, we questioned if this was really what we wanted. No one is ever comfortable admitting they feel like they are going crazy, but hormones can make you feel all kinds of emotions you never knew existed.

During this time, our marriage was also challenged because I wanted to talk about how I was feeling and Ryan didn't. To be fair, Ryan didn't understand how hormones can make a person feel crazy, and I was a walking basket case of hormones. Ugly crying with fists of balled-up Kleenex as though I'd been watch Lifetime movies all day. It was a time when we both needed someone to talk to and talking to each other was not always the best choice. We should have con-sidered couples spiritual direction or couples therapy to sort through our feelings, but because we did not consider ourselves "those kinds of people," we never did so. How prideful of us to think we could suffer and not seek help.

The first round of shots was a fail. The moment I stared down at that first negative pregnancy test, I wanted to vomit. I was so sad and hurt. I just wanted a baby. I was mentally and physically exhausted. The empty feeling of infertility was enough to sink a battle ship, and with each round of shots, my body would overstimulate and my bat-tle ship would sink. I was losing myself in my infertility.

For the health of my ovaries, my doctor strongly recommended putting me on birth control for one or two months after each round of shots, and at the time, I trusted the words that hung on my doctor's lips because I had a singular focus: conceiving a child. I wanted to hold a tiny baby in my arms and experience the love. My desire for a child sometimes felt hijacked by the experiment of fertility. Birth control meant we couldn't try for those months. My body must have been so confused.

I wasn't just physically exhausted. The fertility treatments were exhausting us financially as well. We were working to pay off our mountain of medical bills. Over the course of those three and a half years, we invested so much love, money, and heartache.

During my third round of fertility, we met with the doctor to discuss my follicle count and decide if we were going to undergo IUI (Intrauterine Insemination). Since my follicle count reached a count of ten, my doctor was hesitant about doing the IUI. He told us of the high possibility of conceiving multiples, and if I would get pregnant with a higher number of multiples, there may be talk at some point about selective reduction. I, of course, had no idea what this meant and listened to him explain. My eyes got watery when he compared it to abortion, and my heart sank. How and why would anyone consider doing this? I quickly erased that thought, reminding myself that God would not give us more than we could handle. Two weeks later, I started.

When Ryan and I sat down in our fertility specialist's office after the third failed attempt of fertility shots and IUIs, my doctor looked at us in shock. He didn't understand why I hadn't gotten pregnant. He'd re-examined my chart and told us, "One more time. I think I figured out what is happening with your cycle, my count may have been a day off."

In fertility, hours can matter, so being a day off was significant. We entered round four with only a faint ray of hope after so many times of having a high follicle count and then a negative pregnancy test. This last round of shots proved to be the winning combination of both drugs and time, and we conceived.

I envisioned that when I found out we were pregnant for the first time that it would be beautiful and glorious, but instead I discovered I was pregnant by accident. I was hunched over in extreme pain at home one day not knowing why, and Ryan took me to the ER. They did a pregnancy test as a precaution and the test came back positive. After they reviewed my labs, they sent me directly into an ultrasound to make sure the baby was inside my womb and not in my fallopian tubes.

As they searched on the screen, they told me the baby was in my womb, but that I was over-stimulated from the fertility medication and all my fluids were dumping into my third spaces, causing extreme swelling, pain, and dehydration. I was admitted overnight so they could drain the fluid and rehydrate me. That day in the ER was both painful and delightful because a baby was the cause of my suffering!

At a follow-up appointment, my doctor performed another ultrasound. On the screen we saw two sacs. Twins! We were so excited, but with the good news came information about possible complications. It felt like every time we were given reason to celebrate, unfavorable news would follow. Each time we entered the doctor's office, both Ryan and I held our breath wondering "what next," and this anxiety was preventing us from being able to just enjoy finally being pregnant.

I struggled with the pregnancy, not only with serious morning sickness for twenty-four weeks straight, but I began to worry about vanishing twin syndrome, congenital birth defects, preterm labor, cost associated with multiples, if I would be able to work, paying medical bills, and on and on.

At around fifteen weeks, Ryan and I registered for a multiples class in Baton Rouge. The class began the following week. Around seventeen weeks, we were told that Emma, twin B, may have an abnormality, and the doctor wanted to do further testing. She had possible a marker for Trisomy 18, which has a high mortality rate in utero or within minutes or hours after birth. She also had a marker for Trisomy 21, commonly known as Down's syndrome.

We opted out of further testing because we would never choose abortion regardless of what any test proved. We also knew that the amnio test had a risk of complicating the pregnancy. These babies were a gift from God and the risk was too great. We knew, no matter what was going on with the babies' health, we were going to proceed with the pregnancy. We held on to total faith and trust in God. As much as we tried to remain positive, though, obstacles just kept coming up.

Sunday, October 16, 2005, at twenty-eight weeks pregnant, I began having contractions. Thanks to what I had learned in the multiples class, I knew I was in labor. We arrived at the hospital at seven that morning and about an hour later, my OB, Dr. K, came and checked me. I was nearly three centimeters dilated and my contractions were escalating.

Dr. K had talked to us about the possibly of this happening, but with me still only being in the second trimester, the potential problems the twins could have decreased the longer they stayed in utero. Dr. K decided I should stay in the hospital until the twins were ready to be delivered, and they were stopping my contractions with magnesium sulfate. She quickly said her goodbyes and went to the nurse's station to give the orders.

I can remember what happened next like it was yesterday. As soon as the doctor walked out of the room, I needed to go to the bathroom. I couldn't get up by myself, so Ryan came around to help me. When I stood, I saw the blood. Fear consumed me. Blood during a pregnancy is always a bad sign.

My sister-in-law ran to the nurses' station and in a matter of minutes, they were prepping me for an emergency C-section. I laid on the hospital bed in tears, scared and trembling as Dr. K began to tell me what they were about to do. My fear had paralyzed me. Her voice faded away and I only saw her mouth moving. The only words I remember came when she got close to my face and said, "The babies may come out not crying, not breathing, and possibly lifeless." I started praying silently as I wept, feeling so alone, even with my family at my bedside.

They placed me on the surgery table and stretched my arms wide on these long metal boards, strapping each arm in place. Naked and afraid, humiliated and feeling so alone, I felt like I was laying my life down for my babies like Christ did on the cross.

At 1:28 p.m. Talon Antoine Breaux was born weighing three pounds, one ounce. He was named after a character on one of our favorite shows on MTV that we watched during the pregnancy. Not the best origin story for a first name, but we decided his middle name would be the strong, Catholic, family name of Antoine, which goes all the way back to Talon's great-grandfather, as well as the great St. Anthony, patron saint of lost items including lost people and lost spiritual goods.

One minute later, Emma Grace was born weighing two pounds, five ounces. She was named for my love of reading, in particular, the classic *Emma* by Jane Austen. Her middle name, Grace, was for my hope that she would always be full of grace, like Mary. At the time, I didn't have a close relationship with the Blessed Mother and had no way of knowing that my walk toward her Son's Sacred Heart would be where I found sanctifying grace. The name Emma Grace fit her personality perfectly.

To our great surprise, the twins were born kicking and crying, bursting with life. God had spared them, and it gave me an ounce of hope for their future. I honestly believed that God would save them from any genetic abnormalities. My faith in Jesus has always been important to me. So, I reasoned, I must be important to Him. I had remained hopeful through my pregnancy, and I begged God to give me a miracle during my delivery.

In that moment, I believed He had.

Chapter Four

TALON'S DIAGNOSIS

"Those of steadfast mind you keep in peace—in peace because they trust in you."

—Isaiah 26:3, NRSVCE

THE NEXT DAY, THE NICU DOCTOR CAME TO MY HOSPI-
tal room and gave us more bad news. Talon had all of the markers of
a chromosome abnormality, and they were testing him for Down's
syndrome. I was shocked.

Throughout my pregnancy, the doctors had been monitoring
Emma, thinking she was the one with complications and possible
abnormalities. The doctors totally got this one wrong. One doctor
even admitted that in twenty years, he had never seen a situation
where the twin with the abnormal markers was born healthy and the
twin with no markers was the one with the chromosomal abnormality. They are doctors, not God.

Our babies were dichorionic twins, which basically means twins
who have their own sacs and usually their own placentas. In our case,
they were fraternal, coming from two different sperms/egg fertiliza-

tions: one male and one female. I tell you this to explain there was no possibility that the doctors got the babies mixed up while performing the ultrasounds. The doctors, even with high-definition ultrasound machines, gave an incorrect diagnosis.

This was not the biggest of the surprises regarding our baby boy's health. Talon suffered from two heart defects. At this point, his heart problems were what most impacted his chance for survival. He needed medicine immediately and possibly surgery.

Much of that time is a blur to me because it was impossible to process so much in a short amount of time. All I can remember feeling after hearing about Talon's heart was hopeless and terrified. I did not understand or know how to react to these complications.

I never thought of myself as someone capable of handling a special-needs child, but God evidently viewed me differently. He chose me to be Talon's mom because He knew my heart. I didn't know what life looked like for a child with Down's syndrome. Worry and fear were engulfing me, and I admit, all I wanted to do was run. I can remember saying, "Not us, God. Not me. I can't do this. I am not strong enough for this." I was grieving the loss of the child Talon would have been, instead of accepting the intense love that a special-needs child brings to a family.

A counselor from the hospital and a lady from the Down Syndrome Association of Acadiana came to speak to us before I was discharged. They both were kind and patiently answered our questions, offered support, and seemed to know just how a diagnosis like this affected families. Never once did either counselor judge my questions, nor did I ever sense their impatience with my incessant crying, because they seemed to understand what Ryan and I were going through. We were mourning the life we expected to have with a healthy boy.

I remained in the hospital with complications from the pregnancy and C-section for five days. My anemia was so severe that Dr. K considered blood transfusions right after surgery. During these days, I had time to think and worry about all the what-ifs. Because I was steps away from the NICU, I would often roll myself in a wheelchair across the hospital to see the twins. Still weak from the C-section, I was mentally drained and sleepy all the time. The health issues the babies were having weren't so obvious to me because I wasn't in my clear mind and my memory was so foggy.

Five days later, on October 21, I was discharged, and while the babies remained in the NICU, Ryan and I went back home to rest and recover. We waited for information from the NICU and shortly after arriving home, received a phone call from the doctor confirming that Talon did indeed have Down's. I began to truly mourn the life he could have lived had he been healthy.

For the next three days, I kept asking God how I would be able to take care of a special-needs, premature baby . . . plus another preemie. *How will I do this? I'm not strong enough to handle this!* I was so scared. I doubted my ability to care for a sick child, to be the mother they deserved, and to provide the level of care they needed. I never doubted that God loved me, but was I being punished for my sins? I was desperate to know why!

After I was released from the hospital, Ryan went back to work and instantly fell into "protector dad" mode. He's always been the strong one when I needed freedom to just feel my emotions, but I realized that he was struggling with not being able to protect us.

During this part of our story, I was totally unreeling from all the news coming in—I wasn't able to lift my head up and look around me. The bad news kept coming. On day thirteen, the doctor told us Talon had an infection that was getting progressively worse. I was still on pain medication from my C-section and numb from the news of his Down's syndrome diagnosis. I felt like I didn't really know what was going on inside that NICU even though I was visiting with the babies every day.

I often forget that I was only twenty-five years old at the time, and I had no clue what typically happened in NICUs or even what it was like to have a child. This was our first pregnancy and everything was new. My head was in a total fog and the lack of communication from the doctors and nurses only added to my cluelessness.

On day fifteen, my mom picked me up and drove me to the hospital to visit Talon and Emma, as usual. I walked into the NICU not realizing I was entering as the mother of living twins, but I would be exiting as a bereaved parent.

When I arrived in the NICU, the nurse ushered me to Talon's bedside. I was alone, my mother had stayed back in the waiting room because of infection protocol. The nurse said to me: "It's not looking good, you should call your family." I looked up at her. Wait, what!

My emotions caught fire, and I raised my voice. "You wait to tell me this at eleven a.m. when I am here alone and you suspected this for some time, but didn't pick up the phone and tell us!" She'd known longer than I had. No one called us . . .

My knees buckled, and I began to rustle around in my purse for my phone, panting and trying not to faint. I don't know how I managed to make the call, but Ryan picked up on the first ring. I told him what was happening and to come fast. Then I called Ryan's sister because she was next door at my doctor's office, the office she has worked at for years. I ran to get my mom in the waiting room, and she joined me inside the NICU as we waited for Ryan and the rest of the family to arrive.

Inside, I was yelling at God. *No, God, this is not what You promised! You promised love and healing when we follow You.* I honestly thought if we followed Christ, that when we needed Him most, He would provide for us. *God, where are You? Can You hear me? Why aren't You healing my son? I need You now more than ever. God, listen to me . . . I need You.*

Silence. Except for the alarms from Talon's crib alerting us that the end was near.

Panic reared up again, and I felt myself growing hysterical. I couldn't do this. I didn't want to be there. I had to get out of that room. Other parents, visiting their infants in the NICU, stared at me while I watched my son dying. The hospital didn't make us comfortable in another room so that we could be alone while he passed. It was like we were on Calvary available for onlookers to witness our horror. I felt completely vulnerable with strangers. The room began to tilt and I remember leaping to my feet and running out a side door, Ryan, who had just arrived, chasing behind me.

I can't recall the words Ryan and I spoke to each other standing in that hospital corridor, but I can remember telling him I couldn't watch Talon die. I couldn't find the strength to do it. Time passed, which felt like eternity, but I'm certain it wasn't even minutes, and I had a strong feeling come over me that Talon couldn't die without his mom and dad beside him. I couldn't leave him, I had to go back. I can't explain the range of emotions that went through me that day, or the days to follow, but what I can tell you is that I became someone I didn't recognize. Like the spell of the Beast in *Beauty and the Beast*, I was transformed into something unrecognizable.

We needed to baptize Talon immediately, so we called our parish priest to request baptism and the anointing of the sick, but we couldn't locate Father. So, the hospital stepped in and contacted a nun who came and baptized Talon.

On October 31, 2005, with my entire family gathered around his NICU bed, Talon Antoine Breaux took his last breath and then was placed in my arms. This was the first time I got to hold his tiny body, and it was lifeless, blue, and beautiful. This was final . . . no miracle, no resurrection. My son was dead.

Talon had lived fifteen days. He had blue eyes and blonde hair and would smile at me when I talked to him. I am certain it was not gas. It felt as though our souls knew each other. God had given Talon to us to expand our hearts, although it was years before I had the clarity of mind and spirit to see this. He was the sweetest baby boy that I've ever known. I love him, and I miss him every moment of every day.

While people with children were out smiling, laughing, having fun trick-or-treating, I was holding my dead son in my arms, like Mary held her son Jesus after the Crucifixion. Grief descended and crushed my world; my heart was rumbling like an earthquake. I wanted to throw up, I wanted to run. But where could I go to get relief from these feelings?

When the doctor finally came into the room to speak with us, again my mind was in a far-off land. I don't know what he said. I later learned that we can lose our memories during times of intense grief. It's a form of self-protection. I only remember begging the neonatologist, "You have to fight for Emma Grace because I cannot do this again."

I didn't know if I could trust God because I'd begged, and He hadn't answered the way I wanted. I wanted Him to prove me wrong and save Talon and then ask me: "How could you doubt My capability?" I promise I would have cowered in humility like a little loss puppy. I doubted God's love for me. Then afterward, I was angry with myself for doubting Him. I struggled with this for a long time.

In the pits of despair, we were forced to make arrangements for our son. We walked into the funeral home not knowing how we would pay the bill. We'd spent our entire savings on fertility, Talon's NICU bill was already over $150K, and Emma's was climbing day by day. Talon had no life insurance because you can't get life insurance on a child born unhealthy. The reality of the funeral costs was only making my anxiety more paralyzing.

My sweet husband, trying to stay strong for both of us, let me do what I needed to do. He understood that my grief was different than his. I'd carried Talon inside my womb, and my womb was now empty and my baby was dead.

The funeral home director gave us options, but only one made sense to me. When the funeral director turned the paper around with the price, the blood drained from my face. Upon seeing my reaction, my in-laws, who were kind enough to go with us, asked no questions and wrote the check. This was the only way they knew how to make our suffering a little bit lighter. I'll never forget that they did this for us because we needed their charity more than anyone knew at the time.

It became important to me that everyone know Talon had existed, and that he was a beautiful, perfect child of God. He had ten perfect little fingers and toes. I wanted to make sure he would never be forgotten. I wanted to share our grief with our friends and family—I needed compassion and empathy—and for everyone to see his tiny body and enter into this with us.

Ironically, as much as I wanted to share this experience, at times the funeral got to be just too much, and I would slip into the dark, empty parlor next door to escape. I was still healing, trying to keep up with my breastmilk, acting hormonal, and basically feeling like I was going crazy. But at the time, in my mind, my actions made sense. Grief has a strange way of making you feel ten emotions at once.

Someone suggested that because we didn't have many pictures of him that we should take some there at the funeral home. I snapped back, "Of course not!" and was aggravated that anyone would ask. In no way did I intend to hurt my friends and family, but because of my broken heart, I was lashing out at the people I loved most in this world. So instead of comfort, I would get silence. They became afraid to say anything wrong. This is so sad to realize now.

I did not know how to process this grief, and I didn't know what to do with the pain. It was utter self-destruction. My family stayed in the suffering with us, because they loved us and wanted to continue to walk through this with us, but we weren't always easy to love. There were so many Ruths in my story that I didn't say "thank you" to until recently. I'm ashamed to say that my lack of charity caused pain and suffering for the people who were just trying hard to love me.

> But Ruth said,
>> "Do not press me to leave you
>>> or to turn back from following you!
>> Where you go, I will go;
>>> where you lodge, I will lodge;
>> your people shall be my people,
>>> and your God my God.
>> Where you die, I will die—
>>> there will I be buried.
>> May the Lord do thus and so to me,
>>> and more as well,
>> if even death parts me from you!"
>
> When Naomi saw that she was determined to go with her, she said no more to her.
>
> —Ruth 1: 16–18, NRSVCE

Chapter Five

EMMA'S CONDITION

"As a mother comforts her child, so I will comfort you."

—Isaiah 66:13, NRSVCE

AFTER TALON'S FUNERAL, WE DROVE TO THE HOSPItal to visit Emma. We entered the NICU, trying our hardest to keep it together, but I know we looked distraught. The nurses greeted us with the news that Emma, too, now had an infection.

My heart sank to my feet. Not her too. *God, why? What did I do to deserve this continued pain?* I was fighting back hopelessness, but it was weighing hard on my soul. My faith was wavering. I had been trying for so long to be hopeful, but when I heard about Emma's infection, a storm started brewing in my heart. There was so much fear attached to this news, and I uttered the words "Emma too" and began to weep.

A week later, after doing a CT scan of Emma's heart, the doctors unexpectedly came across an aneurysm on her descending aorta. We met with the pediatric cardiologist, and he gave us the grim report.

Her aneurysm was large, and when I asked him to "give me the size," he responded, "If she were an adult, it would be the size of a grapefruit." Imagine a blood-filled sac on the main artery coming out of your heart the size of a grapefruit!

The doctor told us she wouldn't survive if the aneurysm ruptured, and she required emergency surgery. Because the rarity of this condition and the forty percent mortality rate, we needed an experienced surgeon.

The cardiologist quickly sent off Emma's records to five of the leading children's heart hospitals in the country, being very selective about the surgeons. Boston Children's, Texas Children's, Cincinnati Children's, Cook Children's, and Children's in New Orleans. The next day we had all five opinions back.

Four of the five doctors reported that Emma would die during the procedure. The exact words out of one of the doctor's mouth were, "There is no way she would survive the surgery."

One brave man, Dr. T, at Cook Children's in Fort Worth, Texas, offered to help Emma Grace. Without the surgery, she was going to die because the sac was growing and would eventually rupture. Holding on to a sliver of hope, we were transported via Teddy Bear Air for cardiac surgery. The team arrived to collect Emma Grace, and immediately we felt a peace come over us.

After arriving, we found out that Emma had three aneurysms and needed all three repaired. Apparently, the CT scan had stopped on the upper part of her body and hadn't scanned her lower areas where the other two aneurysms were located. Dr. T assessed her and scheduled the surgery.

It was an eight-hour surgery on my sweet baby girl, who was

only five weeks old and weighed three pounds, five ounces. For eight hours, I paced the hall outside of the waiting room. I was deathly afraid that the next time the phone rang, it would be to inform us that she had died in surgery.

I continued praying, and each time the phone rang, the nurses told me she was stable and holding on. Dr. T met us in the hallway after the surgery and told us she was stable, but still in very critical condition. We needed to wait twenty-four hours to see how she would respond.

I leaped forward, wrapping my arms around his neck, and sobbed, saying "thank you, thank you, thank you." He looked exhausted, like he had just shoveled dirt for eight hours in the Texas sun with no break. I'm sure I freaked him out, but I felt pure love for this stranger who had beat the odds and given Emma a chance to survive. He had given us hope and more time with our daughter.

She spent two weeks in Texas and was finally released to come back home to our local NICU to grow, with only one complication. The right iliac aneurysm had clotted after surgery and the tool to remove the clot was bigger than her artery. Our only option was to leave the clot alone and try to dissolve it with blood thinners. These blood thinners were given twice a day via injections in her legs. We had no idea this complication would eventually be as big of a setback in her development as it turned out to be.

On December 12, we flew back to our local hospital in Louisiana where Emma needed to gain another pound before she could go home. It took her about three weeks to get there, but on January 9, 2006, after eighty-five days in the NICU, she finally came home. With all her setbacks, she actually did very well, coming home only three days after the twins' original due date of January 6, 2006, the Feast of the Epiphany.

Emma was discharged with ten different medications, one that was given as a shot twice a day; she was on oxygen twenty-four hours a day; she had a special neonatal formula as well as a halter monitor that tracked her breathing. I was fearful that something was going to happen to her. What if I gave her the wrong medicine at the wrong time? What if she stopped breathing? What if she needed me, and I didn't hear her? Fear gushed over me like a tidal wave, and I began throwing up, not sleeping, and struggling to eat. After realizing I had lost eleven pounds that first week Emma was home, my OB prescribed me an anti-anxiety medicine.

When people would tell me, "Kelly, you are so strong," I didn't believe them. I was battling anxiety, and it felt like war most days. I wasn't strong, I just didn't have any other options to choose from. I had a child who needed me, and she deserved for me to be a good mother. It was a decision every day: sink or swim. Some days I had my head above water, but even then, I was literally hiding in my house, afraid that at any moment, something bad would happen to her.

A couple weeks later, Ryan encouraged me to talk to someone, and out of love, begged me to go. Staying home with Emma, petrified within those walls all day every day was depleting me. I desperately needed someone to talk to. I scheduled an appointment to see a counselor.

I sulked on the drive there. I didn't want to go and tell someone about my pain. I did not want to be vulnerable. I didn't want to share the depths of my grief. And more than all this, I was afraid that my grief may have triggered bipolar disorder, a genetic condition my mother suffered from. I wasn't sure what was going on inside my heart and my head, and it scared me.

I had watched my mother battle with bipolar along with her depression and anxiety. It was not something I wanted to face, so instead I stuffed down my pain. I had feared this my whole life. I did not want my own children to live with a mother who couldn't really mother them. When I met with the counselor, I shared this with her. She decided to test me.

She conducted an initial screening to determine if I was depressed, had post-partum, or was experiencing deep pangs of grief. I had mixed emotions about the screening, but agreed. I was relieved to hear it wasn't depression or post-partum, but confused as to what was going on.

I learned I was suffering with a delayed reaction to my grief of losing Talon and the anxieties of caring for a sick child. She called it Complicated grief. I didn't know how to fix my grief or work through the fear. As women, we want resolutions, and I couldn't fix this. I was just going to have to endure the pain and suffering and try to work toward healing.

After about six sessions with the counselor, I quit going. In a good attempt to help me, she was trying to compare, in a loving but very impersonal way, her divorce to my grief over child loss. I got angrier every time I thought of it. She was the professional getting paid, and I could have schooled her on what *not* to say to a mother who just lost a child.

I tried going to the grief-sharing group Compassionate Friends, but it just did not work for me. Ryan was okay with the layout, but I didn't like the focus that the circle put on me. I felt isolated as the "new parents," and I'm uncomfortable with people I don't know looking at me. Grief can make every situation feel isolating. Remember, I feel self-conscious crying in front of people. I ugly cry and can't stop. I wasn't ready at that point to be vulnerable with a group of strangers.

Tears are beautiful and are meant to purge the soul. Crying shows our humility, humanity, compassion, and weakness. Jesus wept when he heard that his friend Lazarus had died. But I felt so broken and weak, I couldn't see beyond the grief, and I wasn't ready to share my losses at that support meeting. I should have given them a second chance, but I wasn't very charitable to anyone at this stage of my grieving.

Chapter Six

EMMA, A LIGHT INTO THE WORLD

"Again Jesus spoke to them, saying, 'I am the light of the world; he who follows me will not walk in darkness, but will have the light of life.'"

—John 8:12

AS THE WEEKS PASSED, I BEGAN TO FEEL AND ACT more normal. The anti-anxiety medication was working and allowed me some sense of peace. I was able to go to doctor's appointments with Emma and actually retain the information the doctor was telling me. My mom would come for a visit and we'd ride into town to walk around the stores, just so I could get out of the house. In a reversal of roles, she was my Ruth.

When Emma was ten months old, they were able to take her off of oxygen during the day, and we scheduled her baptism. We had already taken the baptism class when I was pregnant, so we were able to schedule the date quickly and planned the day of celebration with our family.

On September 10, 2006, Deacon Davis poured the water over her little head and said the words, "I baptize you in the name of the Father, and the Son, and the Holy Spirit." With those words spoken, Emma Grace became the Lord's. Deacon Davis took Emma Grace into his arms and lifted her to the heavens, presenting her to the Father. I have the cutest picture of her with her feet and hands together in the air as Deacon Davis held her up. She looks like she's rejoicing.

Emma was a happy, sweet girl. She had some setbacks, but we pushed through them and moved forward. I stayed home with her and tried my best to help her progress. I would take Emma to her appointments, organize and administer her medications, and get creative with ways to get her to gain weight. My brain was on nurse duty 24/7, and sometimes I put so much effort in keeping her alive, that I forgot how to be just a mother to her. It was a hard balance.

Emma needed me. I knew her better than anyone. I could predict her reoccurring sickness; I knew what to do and who to call. But there's a danger to not having an outlet for this level of stress. The saying is true, a mother's love is like no other. But the consequence was that, as much as I fought to keep Emma healthy, my soul suffered. I was starving for Christ.

So many things happened to Emma, many I'm unable to recall with clarity, but when she was about twelve months old, we noticed that her right leg was affecting the way she stood. The clot in her right iliac had dissolved, but there was a possibility that the clot had done damage to her growth plate. If the growth plate was damaged, it could stunt the growth of her right leg and become a problem as her leg continued to grow. We decided we would have to consult an orthopedic surgeon to better address the issues she was facing.

At the orthopedist, they took x-rays and measurements so they could start tracking the growth. She wasn't walking yet, so they didn't recommend any immediate action to remedy the issue.

Six month later, when Emma was eighteen months old, we returned to the orthopedist. She had just begun to walk, and I noticed that the difference in her two legs was starting to affect more than just her standing, but her overall balance. At this appointment, we were told that her right leg length was approximately one inch shorter than her left, and the doctor advised that we see a physical therapist to have her fitted for a special shoe. We were sent home after scheduling a follow-up for six months later.

We made the appointment with the physical therapist to have her fitted for a special shoe so her legs would be the same length, and she could have balance when she stood. We purchased a normal shoe and they added height to it.

Six more months passed and the orthopedist was worried that the growth difference was not slowing down, but progressively getting worse. By the time she was two and a half years old, they measured her right leg as two inches shorter than her left. She wore a shoe that was lifted so that she could get around easily, but at some point, they would not be able to correct this issue without it affecting her knees and hips.

The word *amputation* also came up during this visit. I immediately told the orthopedist no, I was not even going to consider it. No way would I let them do that to my child. I didn't want her to suffer the pain. Some of it was vanity, but most of it was trying to protect her. People would look at her differently, she may not fit in, they may pick on her. I made the best decision I could at that moment. Emma did not let her shorter leg affect how she got around, and boy did she get around.

She was truly filled with grace as her middle name suggests. She was a happy and joyful toddler. She would ask strangers what their name was and where they lived. And like her daddy, she was a natural evangelizer. She would sing "Jesus Loves Me" all the time, brought smiles to people's faces, and poured her little soul into being in the moment wherever she was. Her disability never stopped her, and I think the grace that God gave her was the ability to love whoever was in her presence.

Since I wouldn't consider the amputation, I wanted a second opinion. I started researching and found a reputable doctor in Dallas. After examining Emma, his prognosis was the same. They couldn't improve on her quality of life without amputating her leg and getting her a prosthesis. I said no and we left.

Back at home, I began a more in-depth online search. I eventually found a doctor in Baltimore, Maryland and began reading more about him. Patient after patient shared their successes after being treated by him. After a few weeks, I decided to schedule an appointment.

Dr. P had developed a leg-lengthening procedure. He had successfully lengthened dozens of children's limbs of all different diseases and diagnoses. Finally, with something we could do to help her, I had hope, and I held onto this hope to help my daughter.

After speaking to his office about Emma's condition, they felt she was a candidate for the surgery. The next step was for Dr. P to examine her personally to make sure she didn't have any underlying issues that would cause complications.

I remained faithful to prayer every night for the healing of my sweet girl's leg. My whole life had become doing all I could for Emma's health and well-being. My days were filled with doctor's appointments, physical therapy appointments, occupational therapy, speech therapy, dietician appointments . . . I gave Emma my all, and that's what she needed from me.

All you want is for your child not to suffer, and Emma had suffered an awful lot during her first three years of life. As for me, I could tell there was a lot happening inside that wasn't good. The fear, anxiety, and darkness was clouding me. I was suffocating inside.

There are so many moments while writing this book that my memory just shuts me down. Emma's screams from the many times we had to draw blood to check levels of medication. The multiple CT scans and MRIs. The look in her eyes when she just wanted me to make them stop during gut-wrenching physical therapy sessions. I wanted to steal her away. I wanted all the pain to leave her tiny body. I wanted her to be renewed in Christ, but I didn't ever think there was an end in sight that matched what I had in mind. I wanted her healed, but no option was free of suffering.

I wanted her to be a normal baby, to grow and hit normal milestones. I became envious of others parents whose kids never had to endure a trial. Families who had babies and came home to a normal routine. Who never had to think about how they were going to pay the next bill, or decide which bill to pay first so that the medical care wouldn't be interrupted. Even simple things like how we were going to buy groceries. I was too proud to ask for help. What I needed was humility.

I didn't have much time for my husband or myself. My faith was hanging on by a thread. We went to church, but we were only warming a pew. I hadn't felt God's presence in a very long time. I didn't understand all the healing, restorative gifts that the Catholic Church provides. No confession, no rosaries, no family prayer—the list is a mile long of what we weren't doing. What I leaned on at this point in our journey was a simple prayer: *Jesus, I need You. Jesus, please heal Emma Grace. Lord, I'm struggling.*

Meanwhile, the bills for Emma's medical care kept coming in and they were astronomical. Every time I turned around, there was another doctor bill to pay. The medical bills for Talon and Emma Grace were over $300K. Just when we would pay our deductible for the health insurance, another bill would arrive from a procedure or medication. Most months we had to decide which doctor to pay based on when we had our next appointment with them. We had to keep the bills paid so Emma Grace could get the medical attention she needed moving forward. We didn't qualify for any government insurances or aid. My husband made just over the limit to qualify us, a limit that is doable if you don't have a very sick child that requires extensive medical attention.

I don't know how we made it some days. We lived paycheck to paycheck, and sometimes to be able to eat, we would buy groceries using the credit card. As time passed, nearly everything we needed was bought using credit cards. The financial aspect of her medical situation was a huge burden to our family, and we struggled. We did not have another option and we needed help.

We didn't share these details with our families. We suffered in silence and our marriage was bending under the strain of all the weight.

Chapter Seven

THE RAINBOW

"God said, 'This is the sign of the covenant which I
make between me and you and every living creature
that is with you, for all future generations.'"

—Genesis 9:12

THE VERY NEXT MONTH, I WAS AT WORK AND I REAL-
ized that with all that was going on, I hadn't noticed until that moment that I had missed my period.

I went to Walgreens during lunch. I had never taken an over-the-
counter pregnancy test that came out positive. So, with low expectations, I called my best friend to talk about it while waiting for the re-
sults. It never occurred to me that this test could actually be positive.

We waited, the minutes feeling like hours, for the test to show
the negative sign. Wait for it . . .

Well, I was the one who was surprised, because for the first time,
I was holding a positive pregnancy stick. I hung up the phone and
called Ryan.

Finding out I was pregnant was shocking, and although I was excited that we'd been able to conceive on our own, I was scared out of my mind. How was I going to have a new baby and care for Emma, who needed my undivided attention day and night for her medical care? I had no idea what God was preparing me for. I had no idea how he was stretching me.

Three months later, we held a benefit for Emma and were able to raise the money for all of us to fly to see Dr. P, the orthopedist, for the limb-lengthening surgery on her leg. The surgery would require us to remain in Maryland for six months while she healed and rehabilitated.

This meant that me, Emma, and the new baby would be separated from Ryan. During this pregnancy, we sold our house so we could afford to lease an apartment when Emma had her surgery, and we moved into a mobile home behind Ryan's grandmother's house.

We were making big, life-changing decisions every day it seemed, and it was difficult to know if we were making the right ones. I would pray, but it felt like I was either begging God or hollering at Him. There wasn't one decision I made during this time that brought me peace. We just decided and then prayed it was the right one. I wish I'd known during this hectic time about the Adoration Chapel and what was inside.

The fear and the worry set in and became a huge part of who I was. I was fearful that every decision I made was wrong. I was fearful that Emma would die. I had no idea how we were going to be able to provide financially for all of her medical issues. I questioned everything, because I was having trouble trusting anyone, including myself.

Instead of turning to God in these moments and going deep into my faith, I just existed. I would pray, but I wasn't participating in any sacraments. It felt like graces were just bouncing off me instead of penetrating. If I knew my faith like I do now, I would have been in daily Mass, going to reconciliation, and getting Emma the anointing of the sick. I would have been practicing holy acts such as fasting, praying novenas, saying rosaries, and leaning on my priest for support during this dark time.

I now know how merciful the Father is, and I know that He was close to us, because no matter what happened, somehow, we survived every obstacle that was thrown our way financially and even the hardest decisions were made. We tried our best to just trust.

No one should plunge into the depths of this kind of darkness without being accompanied by Christ. "We know that all things work for good for those who love God" (Rom. 8:28).

On January 6, 2006, my sweet, chubby, healthy girl Estelle Gabriella was born, weighing seven pounds, nine ounces of pure baby perfection. At the time, I didn't realize the significance of her name or the date of her birth. I was due for the twins on January 6, so it was a surprise when I realized I delivered Estelle on their due date, but I was even more surprised to learn the meaning of her name. Estelle means "star," and she was born on the Feast of the Epiphany, which is the feast of the Magi visiting our Lord after His birth. The star points North toward Christ. Finding out the hidden meanings behind Estelle's name and date of birth was evidence to me that God had His hand in my life the entire time I was suffering and in the times when I felt I was alone.

When Emma was able to see her sister for the first time through the glass window, she uttered to my sister-in-law, "Is that my baby sister?" with total wonder in her voice. She would hold her, hug her, kiss her, and lay with her. They were so sweet together.

I wish, for Estelle, that they'd had more time together. The love that Emma gave her sister was pure and beautiful to witness. Adjusting to two was a little rough, but we were happy in our own little way.

I decided before we left for Emma's surgery that I would make a photo book for Ryan to have while we were away. I scheduled family pictures to be taken of all of us. I so wished I had stuck to my original plan and had those portraits taken, but I wanted to surprise Ryan and snuck the session in with just the girls before we left. This was the last picture that I have of the girls together, other than a few we snapped in Disney. In 2009, not everyone had an iPhone, so the pictures aren't the best quality, but they are precious to us.

During this time of preparing for Emma's surgery, so many emotions ran through our home. I see now how God allowed us this extra time to regain some of our strength from this newest transition from one child to two, before the storm hit shore. It was as if a hurricane was brewing out at sea and we were unaware of its imminent landing.

Chapter Eight

FLIGHT TO SURGERY

"Now when they had departed, behold, an angel of the Lord appeared to Joseph in a dream and said, 'Rise, take the child and his mother, and flee to Egypt, and remain there till I tell you; for Herod is about to search for the child, to destroy him.'"

—Matthew 2:13

ON JULY 13, 2009, ON OUR SEVEN-YEAR WEDDING ANniversary, we packed up our vehicle and left for West Palm Beach, Florida, where Dr. P had recently relocated his practice.

We arrived and unpacked our vehicle into the apartment we had rented for the next six months, and then headed out two days later to meet my sister-in-law at Disney World. Emma and Estelle loved Disney so much, as do most little girls. Emma was all smiles the entire time we were there. We stayed for a few days, and then headed back to the apartment.

The day before Emma's surgery, my mother-in-law and her two sisters came to meet us at the apartment, and we all decided to go to the pool. I had an unsettling feeling that the following day, the day of the surgery, wasn't going to go well. It was a gut-wrenching feeling that I couldn't explain. I felt an urgency to cancel the surgery, but I didn't say anything to anyone, and the next day, on July 23, we took Emma to the hospital where Dr. P performed the leg-lengthening surgery.

That night in the hospital, a couple hours after the surgery was over, Emma spiked a fever and started having febrile seizures. The doctors did not know where the fever was coming from. They did multiple tests, and each test came back negative for infection, bacteria, or virus. This left the doctor perplexed about what was going on inside Emma's body.

It was touch and go that first night, and after multiple seizures, they had to intubate her to dispense the medication to help her stop seizing. We prayed nonstop for her little body to start to heal and for the seizures to stop.

She seemed okay the next day, but she wasn't acting like herself. She slept off and on all day, and it was impossible to keep her fever below 104.9. The next morning, July 26, Emma woke up and asked me, with the sweetest expression, as she did every morning, "Mommy, where are we going today?" I said, "Sis, we aren't going anywhere, we are staying here today." She closed her eyes and said, "Okay" and then opened them back up and looked me straight in my eyes. "Mommy, I love you so much." Her words pierced my soul. Those were the last words I heard my daughter speak, the last time I heard her sweet voice.

Within a week of her surgery, she was diagnosed with H1N1, Swine Flu, and the doctors told us she would not survive unless she was transported to Miami Children's via MedJet to be placed on a heart/lung machine called ECMO. We aren't certain, but Emma may have contracted H1N1 during our time in Disney World from someone who was a carrier of the virus.

It was a miracle that Emma even survived the flight over to Miami Children's after coding on the helicopter twice. When we arrived at the hospital, it was touch and go, but by the grace of God, she was put on the ECMO machine successfully.

For seven weeks, we saw every specialist under the sun. It was minute by minute for the first few days, and then it changed to a daily outlook. Each morning we would meet with the doctors as they made rounds, and each morning we had hope that today was going to be a good day.

During this time, Emma overcame a few infections and was making progress with her lungs. Swine Flu, like traditional influenza strains, is a viral infection that causes coughing that in serious cases can turn into pneumonia, lung infections, and breathing problems. The whole time we were in Miami, Emma was in a medical-induced coma so her lungs could heal. I would sing to her, sponge bathe her, and kiss her all over, but we were not able to communicate with one another.

Ryan's mom was able to stay with us for six of the seven weeks we were in Miami. It was hard being away from Estelle, but thankfully, Emma's godfather came to Miami for a visit and brought Estelle with him so we could spend a weekend together. I missed both of my daughters so much during this time: Emma's unresponsiveness and Estelle having to stay back in Louisiana.

Emma fought hard for seven weeks. Ryan and I stayed on our

knees the entire time, begging God that if He saved her, we would never walk away from Him. I remember one of my prayers clearly: "God, You healed Jarius' little girl, why not heal mine? Lord, just say the words *Talitha Koum*. Just tell Emma to rise, if You say it, Lord, she will be healed."

I was hysterical thinking of living my life without her. I couldn't lose another child, I knew if I did that I would go down a path that would be impossible for me to recover from. I wanted to trade places with her, and I begged God to take me instead. I didn't want her to suffer any longer.

But He remained silent, and as the days progressed, so did the disease. It never occurred to me to pray for God's will. I wanted my daughter healed, I did not care at that time what God wanted. I just couldn't lose her, because I knew that if I did, I would die inside.

I remember the day I was standing outside, speaking to my sister on the phone, and I had this feeling come over me. In that moment, I knew what the outcome would be. I blurted, "Emma is going to die." My sister told me to stop it, to not say that, and to hold on to hope, but in my heart, I knew that was not His plan. He was preparing me for the next week, her final week.

I have a vivid memory embedded in my mind of the hospital room where Emma laid hooked up to the ECMO machine. Three poles with IV bags hanging from them, dispensing ten different medications on schedule to keep her body alive. The ECMO pump taking the unoxygenated blood out of her body and re-oxygenating it. It bypassed the heart and the lungs to allow them time to heal. This was where she fought the fight of her life to live.

That week I took my time washing Emma. I cleaned every inch

of my sweet girl, washing her gently with the sponge and massaging her tiny body with lotion. It was a beautiful feeling being able to care for her in this way. After that much time in the hospital, her body needed serious TLC. It made me think of when Mary washed Jesus after the Crucifixion.

Emma continued to fight that week, but on September 10 at one a.m., we received the call that we needed to rush to the hospital because she had taken a turn for the worse. The staff had gotten to know us, they knew our story. When I opened the door to the PICU that early morning, I could hear them praying from the hall as I approached her room. The entire team of nurses were praying over her continuously. They prayed the Our Father, the Hail Mary, and the Glory Be on repeat, begging God to heal this precious child. That day, they entered into the suffering with us. I was so moved by the nurses' prayers and petitions to God.

Our family flew in. My sister, my sister-in-law, my mother-in-law, my dad, my step-mom, my nephew and his girlfriend (now wife) all came in because we did not think she was going to live through the night. The ECMO machine has two tubes that go into the main arteries in the neck, and for some reason, one of them had come unsewn from the inside and she was bleeding out.

The longest day of my life was watching my daughter lie lifeless on the bed, dying, so swollen from the many attempts to save her, my legs barely able to stand because I was so weak from no sleep and no food. I couldn't eat because I couldn't stop throwing up.

As much as we all prayed, and as much as they tried, the doctors couldn't save our daughter, and around seven p.m., her heart stopped.

And so did mine.

For the second time in my life, one of my children had died before my very eyes. I screamed, my heart felt like it was being ripped apart. I called to God, but I heard nothing. *Why are You silent, Lord?*

They took her off all the machines, cleaned her, and placed her into my arms, calling to mind *The Pieta*, the famous sculpture by Michelangelo of Mary holding Jesus after the Crucifixion. I couldn't stop crying. I could not believe what had just happened. My Emma Grace was gone. I was now not just grieving one child's death, but two.

When it was time to leave, I felt so angry with God that when I entered the elevator, I screamed at the top of my lungs: "I hate You, God!" and fell to the floor sobbing. Where was He? Why had He let this happen? I felt sick to my stomach; I needed to vomit.

Back at our temporary apartment, my husband put me in the shower and bathed me as I sat like a zombie, unable to physically do anything but cry. My sister and sister-in-law brushed and blew dry my hair and gave me some Tylenol because my head was pounding. I sat there, silent, and let them dress me. Then they literally tucked me into bed. I felt like a child. For the first time in my life, I was only an empty shell, no charm, no personality, it felt like my soul had left me, and I was lifeless.

I slept, and slept, and slept as they packed the entire apartment back into our car so we could go back home. I couldn't do anything. The next morning, Ryan had to go to the hospital to sign the papers for the funeral home to embalm Emma, because you cannot cross state lines without being embalmed, and we needed to arrange to fly her body back home.

I slept off and on the entire nineteen-hour drive home. I kept thinking about that moment on the elevator when I told God I hated Him—when it felt like He had forsaken me. Those words still haunt me today, though I have confessed and received absolution for saying it. I shouldn't have blamed God for taking Emma back home. I just didn't have the strength to endure this pain again. I didn't even have the desire to try. Even when Talon passed away, my faith wasn't shaken like when Emma passed away. The experiences were very different.

Most of us would do anything to avoid death. See doctors, take this medication, try this experimental drug, consider this treatment, try it all. I didn't want Emma and Talon to died. I tried to avoid death for them and to prevent my own suffering. In enduring the death of my daughter, I understand in a new and deeply profound way how Christ *chose* to endure the pains of a physical death, bearing the weight of the world's sin. I felt Mary's sorrow at a depth that I couldn't understand until losing Emma.

Christ's suffering and death on the cross consoled me as I began to process Emma's death on that long car ride home. *My God, I'm so sorry I ever questioned Your love for me.*

St. John of the Cross would describe these days as my "dark night of the soul," and I can attest to feeling like my soul had gone completely dark the night Emma left earth. I believe God allows us to endure this dark night without emotional and spiritual comfort so that we may expand our hearts and cling to the cross.

When we arrived back home, I ran to my baby girl Estelle and held her in my arms. What a gift it was to have an infant to come home to when my heart was so shattered. What a blessing it was that during all these weeks tending to Emma, our family in Louisiana had been caring for Estelle. They stepped up and loved on her like she was their own.

Over the next few days, we prepared for Emma's funeral. Many family members came to spend time with us, to help us make all the little decisions that are overwhelming when you lose a loved one. One moment stands out in stark relief amid all the grayness of those days. While we were getting photographs together, a friend of ours said, "Kelly, did Emma die on her baptism date?" I ran over to her stack of photos and stood in complete shock.

She had died three years exactly from the date of her baptism, September 10.

Part Two

THE HEALING JOURNEY

"Late have I loved you, Beauty so ancient and so new, late have I loved you! Lo, you were within, but I outside, seeking there for you, and upon the shapely things you have made I rushed headlong—, I misshapen. You were with me, but I was not with you. They held me back far from you, those things which would have no being, were they not in you. You called, shouted, broke through my deafness; you flared, blazed, banished my blindness; you lavished your fragrance, I gasped; and now I pant for you; I tasted you, and I hunger and thirst; you touched me, and I burned for your peace."

—*The Confessions*, Book 10, Chapter 27,

St. Augustine of Hippo [2]

[2] *St. Augustine. The Confessions of St. Augustine. New York: Image Books, 1960.* (Translated into English, with an Introduction and Notes, by John K. Ryan.)

Chapter Nine

BAPTISM

"Go therefore and make disciples of all nations, baptizing them in the name of the Father and of the Son and of the Holy Spirit, teaching them to observe all that I have commanded you; and lo, I am with you always, to the close of the age."

—Matthew 28:19–20

BOTH OF MY CHILDREN HAD DIED ON THE DATE OF their baptism. I never stopped to think about what this meant until after Emma passed away. Then I realized there must be some significance to it.

Our priest told me that some of the saints had died on their baptismal date. I was reminded of this again recently when I heard Pope Francis talk about the importance of knowing our baptismal date. He said, "To know the date of our baptism is to know a blessed day. The danger of not knowing is that we can lose awareness of what the Lord has done in us, the memory of the gift we have received. Thus, we end up considering it only as an event that took place in the past—and not by our own will but by that of our parents—and that it has no impact on the present. Baptism Christifies all who receive it by making us another Christ." [3] It was evident on the day of Emma's baptism that it was her call to holiness. She lived out her little life for Jesus.

At the time, I wasn't in a place emotionally or spiritually to understand the true meaning of the baptismal promise I made on her behalf. At the time, I thought baptism was just something we did in the Church to unite ourselves with God. Now I understand that our baptisms have deep meaning. I was anxious to know why God chose to take them back to heaven on what had been a momentous date in their short lives on earth.

It isn't common to reflect on our children's baptismal day, but we should celebrate this day every year. But when it's the same date that they died, it takes on greater significance. Baptism is the most important day of our lives. This is the day we become a new person, when we receive a new identity. When the holy water is poured over us and the words are spoken: "In the name of the Father, and of the Son, and of the Holy Spirit," we lose the stain of original sin. This is the moment when, like at Jesus' baptism, the heavens are torn open and the Holy Spirit comes down upon us like a dove. Jesus heard the Father's voice say: "This is my beloved Son, with whom I am well pleased." (Matt. 3:17). On the day of their baptisms, Talon and Emma became beloved children of God.

Before their deaths, if a person had asked me why I baptized my

---

[3] "Remember the Date of Your Baptism" written by Devin Watkins, 01/13/19. https://www.vaticannews.va/en/pope/news/2019-01/pope-francis-angelus-remember-date-of-baptism.html. Accessed 10/10/19.

babies, I would have fumbled in giving a complete response. It isn't common to think twice about the date, who the celebrant was, or to meditate on the eternal weight that baptism has on our infants.

Our baptisms made us pure, and confession keeps us pure. The sacraments heal us; they give us the graces to go on. Celebrate the sacraments as often as you possibly can! Not just when you are hurting or going through a difficult season of life, but *all the time*. If we truly understood the fullness of our Catholic faith, we would never, ever leave Jesus. Your healing matters, and the sacraments are tools that enable the healing of your hurting heart because they impart on you the graces you need to endure.

I am comforted knowing that through their baptisms, Emma and Talon, upon their deaths, became saints in heaven with God the Father, God the Son, and God the Holy Spirit. Knowing this allowed me to focus during periods of deepest grief. I would get sad, and then I would remind myself, I raised saints. I knew nothing about raising saints, I wasn't even trying to be a saint, but I knew they were, and suddenly this realization sparked an interest that I, too, may one day attempt sainthood. Sts. Marie-Azélie "Zélie" Guérin Martin and Louis Martin were the first married couple to achieve sainthood and they raised five daughters who became nuns, one of whom is Thérèse of Lisieux, also a saint as well as a Doctor of the Church. This gives me a greater hope that I may one day join them in heaven as a saint. Pope Francis is noted as saying, "To be saints is not a privilege for the few, but a vocation for everyone."

I may have never truly understood what the sacrament of baptism meant if it wasn't for losing Talon and Emma on their baptismal dates, but after praying and reading about this sacrament, I can say with total confidence that the baptismal promise we make on our child's behalf is the single most important decision we can make for them.

I chose heaven for my children, and I clung to that hope after losing them because of the comfort it brought. I believe God revealed the significance of this to me as a way of answering some of my whys.

Chapter Ten

LONELY

"I feel so lost and alone even when I have people around me. Amidst the laughter and conversations, does anyone pause for a moment to realize that I am tired from the weight of this mask that I put on each morning. Smiling and pretending to be fine when deep down I know I am completely shattered."

—Narin Grewal [4]

WHEN YOU LOSE A CHILD, MANY PEOPLE WILL WANT to offer their support, but unless they've experienced child loss themselves, they may not know what to say. Even Ryan, the person who influences me the most and who experienced the same losses, fell short of words on most days.

Many times, I found myself comforting others when we would talk about Talon and Emma. Friends were often speechless. Losing a

---

[4] Narin Grewal, Touchinsouls.com accessed 8/24/19.

child is the single hardest loss a couple experiences, and no words can properly console someone's heart. But saying "I love you" takes some of the sting away. If you don't know what else to say to a grieving parent, just say, "I love you, and I'm praying for you."

For those of us who have experienced child loss, we know being told how strong we are is the exact opposite of what we feel. I felt more like I was doggy paddling in the deep end trying to keep my head above water, and most days nearly drowning. This deep grief sometimes shuts down conversations, unintentionally. If I'm honest, I wanted to tap out of conversations way before they began anyway. I couldn't focus or talk to people for long. My anxiety was raging; I was so overwhelmed most days by just getting up and getting dress. Feeding Estelle and myself and cleaning the house—if I could just accomplish this—was a good day.

I was consumed by my fears and insecurities. How could I respond to someone trying to comfort me when I felt like I was in a tornado spinning out of control? Would it have been helpful for me to share these feelings? Maybe. But most times I would stay quiet because how could I explain the wreckage that was in my heart and mind?

Friends and family would say things like, "I'm sorry, I can't imagine. I've never gone through this." What I wanted to say back was, "I pray to God you will never know what this feels like." That sounds harsh, and if I had responded the way I wanted to, it would have been selfish. So often I would just say thank you or nothing at all.

The words "You are so strong" inhibited me from taking off my mask. They prevented me from allowing myself to be vulnerable and sharing how I really felt. It stopped me from asking for help when I needed it. I didn't feel like I could say, "Hey, I'm actually drowning here." Or "I'm a hot mess; I don't know how I'm going to make it through the next day, the next hour, the next five minutes."

"Strong" becomes a new standard to live up to. No one would have described me as strong before I lost Talon and Emma Grace, so why now? What had changed in me? The only difference was that I faced hell and fought back. The only reason I was still standing was because I had to. What other choice did I have? Telling the person grieving that "they are so strong"—though a person's intentions are pure—can result in the grieving person feeling more isolated, alone, and misunderstood.

People who are suffering need a safe space to speak the truth, to share their story and their feelings without judgment. That is why it's so important for parents who have lost children to help other families experiencing child loss. We need friends who have experienced this same pain. We need to journey together to make sense of this pain.

For those of you who haven't lost a child, it may be more helpful for you to ask questions that allow the grieving person to share exactly what they need or what they are experiencing that day. Questions like:

How are you?

Can I help you with anything at home?

Can I cook for you or come clean your house?

Can I take you to church?

Can I pray for you?

Do you need someone to talk to?

Do you need someone to go shopping with?

The times that helped me the most were when my friends just came over, or picked me up and took me shopping. It helped when we would go bowling, or to the movies, or dinner—normal activities that did not involve having to share my feelings. I had enough opportunities to share my feelings, some days I wanted to say "No, thank you" and just be me again. Grieving parents need to have friends and family who will just love them through their suffering.

The day Emma died was not when the story ended, just as the story didn't end when Jesus died on the cross. I often sit and think about the times when I was in total despair and knew nothing of a way out. Those days felt like the Triduum, the three days leading up to the Jesus' resurrection: Holy Thursday, Good Friday, and the Easter Vigil. The Church teaches that though chronologically it was three days, those three days are liturgically one day "unfolding for us the unity of Christ's Paschal Mystery."[5] Only for me, the total despair lasted a lot longer than three days.

Ryan drove to the airport the day Emma's body arrived and made sure she was placed safely in the funeral home's vehicle and brought to the funeral parlor. Upon arrival, the staff began to prepare Emma for the funeral.

The next day, the mortician contacted us and recommended we wait a few days for all of the swelling in Emma's body to go down,

---

[5] Catholic Church. "Liturgical Year/triduum," in the *Catechism of the Catholic Church*, 2nd ed. Vatican: Libreria Editrice Vaticana, 2012.

and so we waited another three days. Our entire family needed this time. Family never left our side, and they consoled us the best way they knew how. We leaned on our family and friends for support, for love, and at times, to literally hold us up so we wouldn't fall.

On September fifteenth, we opened the funeral parlor to friends and family. For the first hour, we wept at her casket. I remember thinking, *This is really happening*. It hadn't just been a dream. For the first time, I said aloud, "This is my story, and this will be my life."

My precious girl laid silently in her pink smocked dress and her beautiful pink casket. I asked a photographer to please capture the funeral, which was totally different from Talon's funeral. I do not know why, it's just how I felt at the time. We also hired a horse-drawn carriage from New Orleans to carry her coffin to her final resting place.

It was a beautiful funeral, but just as at Talon's funeral, the people kept coming and coming, and before long, I was feeling trapped at the family couch with a sea of friends and family. All I wanted to do was run and hide. I was so overwhelmed with emotions, all I could think of was getting out of there.

As I had done in the hospital right before Talon passed away, I literally ran . . . out of the funeral home, around the corner, and behind the air conditioning unit. My friends chased me outside to console me, and I sobbed. I was gasping and felt faint. I was struggling to face that this was my new reality. I wanted out; I felt like there was no hope left. I felt abandoned.

It took a while and some convincing for me to gather my composure, and my friends never left my side. They consoled me and talked me through the turmoil in my heart. When I was finally okay to go back inside, they took me to the bathroom where they could clean me up. They wiped the makeup that was all over my face and brushed my hair. I sat and let them try their best to put me back together.

As the time came to say our final goodbyes, I melted in shock and disbelief that this was the end. We had to kiss Emma Grace goodbye, and I wouldn't see her face again until heaven. The horse pulled out of the funeral home to the church, and then from the church to Cemetery #2 in Breaux Bridge, carrying my sweet girl to her final resting place.

I left the funeral home empty. Even though Estelle was my main focus now, I had been Emma's caretaker for so long, it was as if my sole purpose was over, and a deep depression came over me. Research shows that those who lose their role as a caregiver due to death can suffer unresolved grief, long-term PTSD symptoms, loss of meaning in one's life, and the biological impact of severe prolonged stress.[6] I was experiencing all of these.

I wasn't ready to go back home and so Ryan, Estelle, and I remained at my sister-in-law's home for two weeks after the funeral. After those two weeks were over, my family helped us get settled back at home.

Ryan and I are so grateful that our families were mindful about us taking great care with what we did with Emma's personal items. When we got home, we were not ready to pack up her things, so we placed all of her belongings back inside her room and closed the door.

---

[6] National Center for Biotechnology Information (NCBI) "Family Caregiving Roles and Impacts" https://www.ncbi.nlm.nih.gov/books/NBK396398/

Once we were settled back at home, the simplest outings caused me so much anxiety that I avoided going anywhere. In my mind, everyone was staring at me, and I felt like all they saw was poor, pitiful Kelly. When I would look at people, I saw pity and empathy written on their faces, and I couldn't get away from being "the mom who just lost a *second* child."

Nothing made me feel better. Going into public wasn't easy because I wasn't ready to speak with people in the community . . . everyone knew our family and our story. I didn't want to speak about Emma's death over and over again. As kind as people were, each retelling of what happened felt like knives stabbing my heart. I avoided certain places, like the grocery store, parties, and social functions that would allow people to ask about Emma. I just needed some time to get my feet back under me again before I could share anything.

I didn't realize what was happening at the time, but in hindsight, being outside of my home triggered my panic, and so it became traumatic for me to go anywhere. I didn't want anyone to see me cry in public because I wouldn't be able to stop. I stopped going to the cemetery because I didn't want to drown in tears all day. I stopped going to church because sitting in Mass only caused me to replay the funeral over and over in my mind. Or I would see tiny caskets or young girls who looked just like Emma. I would start hyperventilating and I'd have to leave. My church, the place I once loved and felt the Lord's peace, became one more place to avoid.

The severity of the situation was life altering. The world I once knew, the one that radiated in vibrant rainbow colors, was now gray. God's voice in nature stopped. The world became very silent. Everywhere I went would bring up a memory of Talon and Emma and send me down a dark spiral. I no longer felt any of the joy that I experienced daily in my previous life. All I felt now was hollow.

As time passed, everyone's lives went back to normal except for mine and Ryan's. We were stuck in a tornado of sadness, spinning in our own pain and grief. It was hard to watch our loved ones not know how to help us. We hadn't chosen this for our life. Still today we strive to be rid of this cross, but it is our cross, and we are trying our best to run toward Christ with it. Most days, it feels more like we are dragging it along behind us. Surviving the death of your child is the hardest thing a person will ever endure. Trying to do it without God is impossible.

Not long after the funeral, I began having nightmares. I would get in bed at night and close my eyes. I was instantly taken back to the hospital rooms where Talon and Emma lay lifeless on their beds. I could retrace every item in the room, the details are etched in my brain.

The nightmares added another level of chaos to my life because they were preventing me from getting enough sleep. I prayed and prayed to God for the nightmares to end, but they wouldn't. It was like I had a video roll of the days of Talon and Emma's deaths on re-play in my head, and when I tried to press pause or stop, the button would move. It was exhausting.

I let myself just marinate in the pain. I didn't seek the sacraments to begin the healing process. Grief became a giant in my life, and it consumed me. Grief removes a person's ability to think clearly. I was numb and didn't know what step to take next. I would often just stare out of the window at the trees, but not even really see them. I forgot that the trees actually had leaves on them or that the leaves were vibrant shades of green. I forgot that the birds sang in the early morning. I was oblivious to what was going on in the world. I became blind and deaf to life.

My grief had me on a one-way trip to hell. This road was paved with tears, pain, and anger. There was no forgiveness, no love, and no mercy; I didn't want to keep living like this, but I didn't know how to get out.

Fr. Allen Breaux, one of Ryan's relatives, came to our home to check on us a few weeks after Emma passed away. He hadn't seen us in Mass since the funeral and knew we were struggling. He sat us down on the sofa and spoke plainly to us. I don't remember much of the conversation—another side effect of grief is memory fatigue—but there was one thing he told us that I remember clearly. "Your sole purpose as parents is to get your children to heaven, and you've got two of your children there; now you need to get Estelle there."

He spoke those words with such sincerity. I believed him, but the additional pain of going to Mass and what that triggered was more than I could handle at the time. So while I heard what he was trying to tell me, I didn't understand the reality of it until much later.

Days turned into weeks, and weeks into months. Estelle turned two, then three. I was a hamster on a wheel, going through the motions, not thinking about my life or where I was going. I just existed, without purpose.

In those early days of grief, one thing was clear. I didn't fully realize just how much God loves me. Now I truly believe in the depth of His love for me. And over the course of several years, He healed me.

Many events transpired that contributed to my healing. Some of these events felt like set-backs at the time, but even with those, I see now they were lessons about God's heart that I desperately needed to understand.

Though Ryan's words failed to comfort me most times, he was the rock that I leaned on, and occasionally, he would give me access to his grieving heart. My husband is physically strong on the outside, but inside he has a soft heart. He just doesn't show it often, to protect it. He had a hard time processing his feelings about losing Talon and Emma. Before the twins were born, I had only seen Ryan cry on two occasions: the first time was when we were still dating and had our first argument, and the second was when his grandfather died.

When Talon passed away, Ryan's heart melted like a piece of ice in the Louisiana sun, and the tears came and just kept coming. While the tears fell, the words remained stuck. He struggled to communicate with me all of the emotions his heart was feeling. Instead of saying just anything, most days he said nothing. This would often leave me hurting more, because he did not confide in me.

At first this wasn't a huge problem, because I thought that was to be expected. But as time passed, I needed someone to talk to, and Ryan couldn't form the words to help me. I just didn't understand why he couldn't talk to me. When Ryan would say nothing, I felt like he didn't love our children as much as I did. I felt that I was the only one who was grieving in our marriage. There were times when I couldn't hold back my anger, my hurt, my pain—and it hurt Ryan more. Hurt people hurt people, and I felt that I was suffering alone and didn't realize until later that we were hurting each other every day that we didn't choose to grieve as a couple.

Life quickly got very difficult for us the less we spoke about our feelings. It's no wonder that the number one reason for divorce is communication. Especially after the loss of a child, it is vital to communicate with your spouse if your marriage is to survive.

Chapter Eleven

A FATHER'S LOSS

"A father's love is unconditional . . . But almost all
of the time [he] fails to express it."

—Arunima Ravindrakumar

LOSING TWO CHILDREN WAS BY FAR THE HARDEST
thing that Kelly and I have had to endure. Holding Talon's tiny body,
and kissing him goodbye, was excruciating. His casket was so very
small and light that I carried it alone. We lost Talon when he was just
fifteen days old. We never thought this could happen to us. How
could this be our story? It felt that we had climbed into someone
else's nightmare.

I hadn't made praying or attending Mass weekly a priority in a
long time. We would attend "if we had time" and out of convenience
instead of out of love. When I was carrying my son's coffin to the
front of St. Bernard of Clairvaux in Breaux Bridge, Louisiana, it hit
me. This was our home. Every important moment in our life had
happened at St. Bernard, and we should be here every Sunday honoring God and those moments.

Before losing Talon, we thought we had this life thing figured out and that we could be faithful and religious when we were old, when we had more time to devote to it, like my grandmother. It's like we treated our faith as a retirement plan. We were so wrong. In an instant life can change, as it did for us, and it didn't stop changing after burying Talon. Neither Kelly nor I had time to process our grief before shifting our focus back on Emma Grace's survival. Though it should have been, church was not a priority, because were busy making life-altering decisions for Emma's life.

Like most men, I buried my grief because I wanted to be strong for my wife. I wouldn't cry in front of her because I assumed it would make her cry and ruin what might be a good day for her. Most days I cried all the way to work and all the way home. I never shared my pain with Kelly. I stuffed my pain down to protect my wife. This is what I assumed she needed. I was so wrong. Keeping my emotions to myself formed a huge wedge between us because more than ever, Kelly needed someone to talk to. It was my job to be that person, but I failed to show up and be that man. I was the only one who understood what she was going through, and yet I said nothing. I don't know why I felt that she didn't need to talk about it.

Kelly and I were asked to do a marriage talk at a Catholic Church in Franklin, Tennessee, in 2018. I was struggling with the idea of sharing my feelings. I didn't think I would be able to form the words. I asked Kelly to sit with me, to help me write my part.

We sat on our patio one day for three hours and cried together as we wrote what we would say. I was finally able to share how many times I'd failed her during these darkest times in our marriage. As hard as this sharing was for us, it brought us closer than we ever were before. I realized that day that our suffering had the ability to bring us closer together, but we had to be willing to face those hard times and difficult conversations together. It is not only important for our marriage, but for our salvation. Through the sacrament of our marriage, we learned how to love God more fully.

When we lost Emma Grace, I thought, *I didn't know how to do this the first time, much less this time.* Losing Emma Grace was harder on Kelly because of her role as caretaker. It was mentally and physically soul crushing for our family to endure this a second time. Losing a child is unexplainable. Children are supposed to bury their parents, not vice-versa.

One of the most valuable lessons I learned through all this is how important it is to *communicate with your spouse.* We should have taken the two-become-one thing more seriously. Instead, I tried to be her rock, and although she did need a physical rock, she needed a spiritual rock more. She needed someone to pray with, someone to talk to, someone to drive her to church, someone to sit with her in Adoration. I thought I was being strong and helpful. I was doing a lot, but it wasn't enough of what she actually needed. She needed me to be a man, a real man. The man who would protect her physically, yes, but more importantly, would protect her heart.

We didn't ask for this cross, we didn't make choices that led us here; the events were out of our control. But instead of us facing this together, we tried to do it alone. This was a big mistake. Kelly was experiencing severe depression, and all I knew to do was wipe the tears that fell from her cheeks. I thought that being present was enough.

Another lesson I learned is the importance of having a prayer life with your wife and your children. Praying together will bring you closer to Christ and closer as a family. One of my failings is that I would pray nonstop for my family, and especially for Kelly, but I always prayed alone. I never told my wife I was praying for her, and I never asked her to pray with me or join me in my daily prayers.

I didn't ask her about what she was going through, and I didn't share with her what I was going through. The hardest words to hear from your wife when she discovers that you were praying for her the entire time but not including her in your prayer time were, "I feel betrayed." She had desired this intimate time with me and the Lord together, but I never asked her to join me.

I thought I was supporting her, but I was not. We were grieving separately, and this created so much distance. I failed her so many times, because what I thought that she needed wasn't what she needed. I should have asked her. Husbands, if you and your wife are grieving separately, make the effort to begin praying together. It makes all the difference in the world.

Chapter Twelve

OUR HONEY IS GONE

"He will wipe away every tear from their eyes, and death shall be no more, neither shall there be mourning nor crying nor pain any more, for the former things have passed away."

—Revelation 21:4

DURING A STENT IN A FACILITY FOR PATIENTS WHO EXperience severe depression, my mom, who we call Honey, was diagnosed with bipolar disorder just a few months after I was born in 1980. I only remember stories that people have told me over the years, but what I've heard, thank the good Lord, I wasn't aware of at the time. Her illness was triggered from postpartum depression after having me.

My mother suffered with this illness off and on for the rest of her life. She was in and out of facilities during my childhood, but there isn't much that I remember about the onset of her depression. My mother was always the sweetest person who cared more for others than for herself, and so it was hard for others to see her illness. But when the depression claimed her, her personality changed, and she became someone I did not recognize. It's something I will never fully understand, how the brain can do this, but during those short-lived episodes, I had to become someone else as well.

Part of my struggle as an adult stems from the environment I grew up in. Bipolar disorder steals a person's ability to perform normal daily activities. Losing track of time, losing items, breaking things, leaving food in cars, over-spending, forgetting to take medication, not having good personal hygiene, forgetting about dishes and laundry. When an episode was triggered, daily tasks were often forgotten and it lead her to focus extra hard on things that weren't always healthy. Unhealthy spending, binge TV watching, or excessively cleaning areas of the house.

Some things Mom did were beautiful, but it was the time she dedicated to it that wasn't healthy. Often I would find her reading her Bible, and what would take most people months to do, Mom could accomplish in a matter of days.

Her intentions were pure, but these behaviors created problems that were counter-productive to the normal activities of daily living. She would forget to be a mom first, and sometimes my sister Kimberly and I suffered because of it.

My mother's behavior created unhealthy habits for my sister and me. This most obviously manifested in our obsession to raise our children differently than the way our mom raised us. My mom was a beautiful soul, but I had to grow up faster than I should have, and the expectations I placed on myself caused a great deal of anxiety. My sister and I grew to be adults who needed our personal lives to look entirely different than the one we grew up in, and our innocence was the price we paid.

If you dropped by my house today, you'd see a whole lot of order and organization going on. Some of it is productive and some is not. I struggle daily with balancing between the two. The way that I parent is different as well. Our whole life growing up revolved around my mother's illness, and so we rarely were able to participate in sports or extracurricular activities.

In the back of my mind, I held onto the fear that I would one day become like my mom, not able to properly care for my children. As a way to maintain control, I would carefully plot out the direction my life would take. Silly me, I thought I was in control of the outcome. I would look at situations that hadn't gone as I'd planned and wonder what I'd done wrong.

When Talon died, I was terrified that the loss would trigger the onset of bipolar disorder in me. I tried to keep my fear hidden, but there were times when Ryan would just look at me and say, "Kelly, I'm worried about you." Some part of me knew he was right to worry, but I refused to admit it. I was fearful for being judged, even though internally I felt like I was going crazy with all of these emotions. I kept my mouth shut because I didn't want to be labeled "crazy," as some had said about my mother. They were wrong about her; she was one of the mostly loving people I knew, she just had a brain disorder that hindered her from being able to act as a mother first, even after Kimberly and I were grown and married.

It was a harsh reality that left me feeling even worse, wanting to have a mother to run to in this hopeless time of grief, but knowing that wasn't possible. She loved me the best way she knew how, but it was by no means healthy. My mother didn't possess the ability to hold up her broken daughter and help her put the pieces back together. I desperately wanted her to help me figure this out, but she just couldn't, and my heart hurt because I needed her.

In 2006 after wrecking her car, doctors had taken away my mom's driver's license. She lived in a house in New Iberia, LA, which was far for us to travel on a regular basis, so we moved her closer to us. For several years, she was able to live alone and we would frequently drop by and make sure her medication was together, check her groceries, and help with washing clothes. This lasted three years. It was a huge undertaking and we helped Mom as much as we could. But in 2009, while Emma was in the hospital, my mom almost burnt down her apartment. Kimberly and I had to decide what the best plan would be to keep her safe. Both of us had small children, and once Emma grew sick, it fell on my sister's lap to carry the load for us both. She couldn't maintain it alone any longer.

When Emma passed away, I literally checked out. I told my sister I could not help with Mom any longer. I could barely take care of myself and Estelle. I was afraid, with Emma dying and the toll it took on my physical and emotional health, that I had a high chance of triggering bipolar disorder. I couldn't do that to Estelle. My sister and I decided it was time to place my mom in a nursing home, a decision that brought along with it a great deal of guilt, because I desired to care for her but emotionally couldn't.

We completed the paperwork for my mom's interdiction, where a judge declared her unable to care for her own needs. It was a lengthy and expensive process, but the only way we could make decisions on her behalf. My mom had suffered from bipolar since I was born—

twenty-nine years at that point—and for those many years, we were often fixing situations she created. It may have been something she broke or a debt she incurred. It seemed once one thing was settled, something else would happen. It was so bad we eventually had to alert the credit bureau so she couldn't open new credit cards. I'm sure the convicted felon in her apartment complex was sad the day her bank account got additional security precautions since he wouldn't be able to buy any more vehicles in her name. Her judgment was sketchy, and she was always her worst enemy.

Deciding to place my mom in a nursing home came with a heavy heart, but my sister and I felt we had run out of options. My sister's son Konnor was five, her daughter Kaylen was three and a half, Talon and Emma had both passed away, and Estelle was only nine months old.

Nothing in my life has ever been easy. I've always had to work hard or struggle through tough times. When I come across people complaining about their mother, I want to tell them to thank God that their mom is still alive.

My mom wanted to do things for her daughters and her grand-children, but she wasn't always able to. On the days when my mom would come for a visit, we couldn't leave our children with her, even for a minute. But she was so happy sitting with them and just talking and watching them play. She was doing what she could, and it was enough.

Honey lived in the nursing home from 2009 until her death in 2015. The day she died, I had taken her to an eye appointment in town, and we were sitting in the waiting room waiting to be called back. Mom seemed different that day, but her anxiety fluctuated so

I attributed it to that. I thought maybe she didn't want to go, or that she was a little frustrated about something.

By the time I realized what was going on, it was too late. We called 911 and drove around the block to the hospital where they were waiting for us. My mom died of a massive heart attack in the parking lot of the hospital right in front of me.

I have no words for the way I felt that day watching her fight to take her final breaths, and no words for when the doctors couldn't restart her heart. My mom was very ill, but she was my mom and I needed her to love me with that unconditional love a mother has for her child. I needed someone to talk to, and for her to listen as I shared what was on my heart. Even though she was ill, she was a very good listener, she showed true compassion for others and loved deeply.

Honey's death was an incredible loss for our family, and it left us all in a stormy sea of emotion again. The sea was raging, the waves were crashing, and the beach was eroding once again.

Saying goodbye to Honey was difficult for us all, and especially my sister's children, our godchildren, Konnor and Kaylen. Estelle was only six at the time and didn't really understand what was going on. But the faces of my niece and my nephew when we told them what happened pierced my heart. It was difficult to watch my sister, who had been my mother's main caregiver, suffering. It's easier to feel the pain yourself than watch someone you love feeling it.

The hardest part of my healing process for Talon and Emma Grace was that it kept getting interrupted by more loss. Grieving takes time to process. I hadn't completely healed from losing Talon when I lost Emma. Then after Emma passed away, three years later

I miscarried. Then three years later we loss Honey. My grief kept stacking like bricks, creating an impossible weight to carry.

Losing Honey was one of those moments in my life where I fought to find my way back to the surface again. I lost one of my biggest support systems when Honey died. The daily calls to check on me, the prayers, and the love that Honey gave to me, were needed and wanted. I still miss her each day.

Eight days after Honey died was Talon and Emma's birthday. My friend and I had a trip planned to go to the Great Wolf Lodge in Texas. I decided to honor Honey and bring Estelle on that trip. The day we left, which also would have been Talon and Emma's 10th birthday, we stopped in to grab lunch before we got on the interstate. Wendy's had these new cups and on the cups, it read: Happy 10th Birthday, Angel.

I couldn't help but imagine that when Honey arrived at the gates of heaven, three little saints would be there to greet her. Jumping into her arms, they would welcome her home. What a glorious day to receive a sign of hope.

Chapter Thirteen

LOSING ISLEY

"The best way to prepare for death is to spend every
day of life as though it was your last."

—St. Philip Neri

I CAN'T HONESTLY TELL YOU WHAT BEGAN TO CHANGE
my thinking about death and grief, but as time went on, my thoughts
did change. The waves of grief didn't come as frequently, but when
they came, they packed the same painful punch.

The depression and anxiety were intense, and those surrounding
me were the ones who took the brunt of the blows. I was intolerant
of parents who complained about their children. One time I had a
knock-down-drag-out on Facebook Messenger with a woman with
four kids who was complaining about the amount of laundry she
had, and how tired she was being pregnant with her fifth child. Quiet me, who never confronts anyone, messaged this woman. My judgment was clouded by my grief, and it destroyed anyone in its path.

My family walked around on eggshells with me, and I didn't
like the person I had become. I wasn't the joyful, easygoing, quiet

girl who was a deep thinker, loved her family, and loved to organize and read. I had become someone else entirely. I was the epitome of self-destruction. I realize now that the reason I could not get out of my depression, grief, and self-destruction to receive grace was because I was running from God. I was running away from my faith, and I was not visiting the sacraments to receive His grace and mercy. But one day, that all changed.

On April 24, 2016, my friend Misty was traveling home from a Carrie Underwood concert with her ten-year-old daughter Isley. In a split second, their family's lives changed forever when Misty and Isley were hit head-on by a drunk driver who crossed the center line because he did not see the traffic in front of him stopping for a red light.

The vehicle was crushed and afterward looked like a twisted piece of metal. When Misty realized what had happened, she reached for her Divine Mercy card while the paramedics cut her and Isley out of the car. They were both transported to a local hospital, and a little after midnight, sweet Isley entered heaven's gates.

I was oblivious to what had happened until the next morning when another friend called me on her way to the gym. She had heard the news from an outside source, but wasn't exactly sure if Isley was in critical condition or had actually died.

We stayed on the phone for a couple of minutes, and when she walked in the gym, she asked a member who confirmed that yes, Isley had died. I can remember like it was yesterday, I fell to my knees and started screaming. I knew people who had lost children, but never anyone close to me. This hit too close to home. I had lived in a grief bubble, but when Misty lost Isley, I went from treading water in the deep end of the pool to jumping out of the water. My grief was placed on hold, and I needed to call on my experiences with death so I could help their family get through the week leading up to the funeral.

I called a mutual friend whose daughter was friends with Isley. We struggled to talk through the tears, and I think the only words I could utter were: "I'm on my way." I jumped in my car and drove to school.

When I arrived in the parish hall, no one knew what to do. The current administration of our little school had not lost a student before and all eyes quickly fell on me. I hadn't driven to the school with the expectation of helping the children, but I quickly jumped into the role of assigning tasks to administration and the guidance counselor on how to console and comfort the children and what they could do to honor Isley's memory.

God placed me there for a reason. After we separated the girls and boys and assigned the first round of what to do next, a nearby school's counseling team showed up and took over. We left and headed to Misty and Shane's house.

Driving to their house was heartbreaking. I couldn't stop crying and had an instant headache. As I arrived and was walking toward the door, my heart began to beat outside of my chest. It felt like an out-of-body experience. I knew that God was carrying me through each step to face Misty and Shane.

When our eyes met, all I could do was hug Misty, sit, and weep. I wanted so badly to help my friend face the next few days, but I struggled with feeling like the wind had been knocked out of me. We were able to support the family through the funeral by providing food and drinks, but everyone walked around feeling lost and devastated.

I tried my hardest for the first few weeks to be supportive of both Misty and Shane, but I quickly slipped into a depression and regressed. Isley's death hit too close to home, and my grief resurfaced like a tidal wave. I was transported back to the days when we'd first lost both Talon and then later Emma Grace. I walked those steps again, and little by little, I sank deeper. It was the first time in my grief where I realized, because I hadn't faced my giant, that my giant was coming down to face me again.

During this time, Ryan and I experienced a rift with our extended family. As I noted earlier, people's lives returned to normal after a time. One of our family members planned their son's birthday on Emma's heaven day, what we call the day she died; and I was crushed.

Their heaven day is the day we try our hardest to remember each of our children. One of the biggest fears parents who've lost a child have is that their child will be forgotten. We want others to remember them and our loss on this day. It's our day to just be, and however that day unfolds, whatever emotions bubble up, we allow ourselves to just feel them. Allowing ourselves the space and time to do this has been an important step in our healing. It's so important for parents of loss to have permission to grieve and feel all the aftermath of child loss.

Our family member had told me six weeks before the day. I guess it was a way to prepare me, but nothing could prepare me for this, and for the next six weeks, I cried every single day. It is difficult to explain the hurt I felt. It felt like our family was betraying us. I honestly don't think this was intentional, I just think that people don't understand that grieving for your child never really ends.

The date of the death of both Talon and Emma Grace were the hardest days of our lives. It changed who we were and the dynamics of our family. Celebrating another child on that day felt so wrong. We just couldn't do it. We have since talked about it, and we have forgiven each other, but at the time, it ripped me to the core.

Ryan, Estelle, and I did not attend the birthday party, and this was hurtful to the family, but that had not been our intention. We felt that our extended family should have remained sensitive to how losing Talon and Emma Grace changed our lives in such a radical way. Each year without them is a year to grieve the future we wanted to share with them. We also wanted our family to respect our children's lives, no matter how long they lived, and honor their special occasions every year.

But what we failed to remember is that we are human, and our human minds can forget that the pain a grieving parent feels never goes away. Isaiah 49:15 speaks to this very truth. "Can a mother forget her infant, be without tenderness for the child of her womb?" In our humanity, we can forget, especially if it wasn't a direct loss. It will never hurt a grieving parent to honor their child's loss. It speaks love and respect to them. It's not owed, or demanded, but when you love someone, it can make a huge impact on their heart.

Ryan and I could have done more to communicate to our loved ones so they knew how we were feeling, but we were silent. I think for so long it was to protect everyone from the pain that still existed inside our hearts. It wasn't until Ryan received a phone call from his mom that he shared how hurt we were. At that point, weeks had passed and resentment had set it. It was on both sides. I think there was blame that we were being selfish, and as selfish as maybe they felt it seemed, it was never selfishly driven.

One of the hardest parts of grief is finding the words to explain how you are feeling amongst those who do not understand child loss, and here was another casualty of that lack of communication. We thought we were protecting them from our pain, but we were hiding it. So our pain appeared to be gone.

For couples who have lost a child, don't be shy about telling the people who love you what you need regarding things like your child's heaven date. Your family and friends want to love you, but they need your help. It's dangerous to make assumptions and feelings can get hurt.

Another valuable lesson I learned through my grief was to try to have the suffering person's best interest at heart. People may be suffering a lot longer or more deeply than they are letting on. Don't assume someone doesn't want to heal or that they are playing a victim. Everyone grieves differently, and even if they don't show their pain, try to offer your love first. Grieving in public doesn't necessarily mean that someone is weak or if they don't show their emotion, it doesn't mean they are faking it. It simply means everyone is different and recovery time can vary greatly. No matter how hard I try to heal totally, I understand that healing is progressive, and I will stumble many times before I get my feet back on the ground.

Grief is the giant elephant in the room no one wants to talk about. Sometimes people avoid us, and not because they do not love us. I think it is because we are everyone's worst nightmare. Bad things can happen to good people, and our story makes child loss a reality to others.

I will make mistakes and take my family's understanding for granted. Even as much as I hate to admit this, I have done this multiple time. Not because I do not love them, or because I love them too little. It's because grief transforms your heart. It makes you do things you would never dream of doing. You say things that aren't in your vocabulary. You hurt in ways you never knew existed, and speaking those pains out loud is even more painful. Sometimes the best thing to say is nothing. And then one day you are staring at your grief in the face and feeling blindsided that after five, six, ten, fifteen years, you hurt the same.

The journey toward heaven is long and hard, but I've learned that God will pick me up every time I fall and love me for trying. His love and mercy will prevail, if I let it.

Chapter Fourteen

SPIRITUAL SISTERS

"Iron sharpens iron; and one man sharpens another."
—Proverbs 27:17

ISLEY'S DEATH WAS LIKE PERMANENTLY RIPPING OFF a Band-Aid that for so long, I'd just kept replacing. The wound was still raw. But the one positive outcome from that tragedy was that it made me react. Both Ryan and I reacted out of pure love for our friends. Emma Grace had been gone for six years and I'd held it together for as long as I could. But now the dam had broken.

I tried to help Misty as much as I could. I'd take her shopping, bringing her take-out meals, and sit with her. I tried not to offer her too much advice. The way a child dies can change the way a parent grieves. Since my children weren't taken away from me by someone else through a tragic accident, I could share some things, but the grieving wasn't the same.

I noticed I was grieving differently than Misty and, at first, I thought it may have been because our children's deaths came about from such different circumstances. Then the truth came to me. I was grieving from a place where Christ wasn't present. Misty was sharing her grief with Christ. You can't give what you don't have. My heart wanted to help, but I first needed to help myself. I wanted to love her through her loss, but I realized that it had to come from a place of healing. You cannot love in an authentic way unless you have encountered Christ. My desire to know Christ was starting to grow. The seed planted long ago was starting to take root.

I didn't need to wait until I was healed to help Misty, but I needed to know where to find that healing. It wasn't enough to know of God; I needed to know that He was my Father. I needed to have a personal relationship with Him.

Misty and a mutual friend, Ashley, had started a small women's church group right after Misty came home from a retreat called Cursillo. Cursillo (ker-see-yo) is the Spanish word for "little course in Christianity" and it is a three-day walk with the Holy Spirit where clergy and laypeople give a series of talks about the Catholic faith. That September 2016, our prayer group formed. My dear friends just listened as I talked about my heartaches, and we would cry often, but it is during these grouping times that I began what I call my "reversion" back into Catholicism. It was when I began my transformation from Saul to Paul; where I wasn't just warming a pew, but felt a belonging.

During these prayer group sessions, we would talk about events that had shaped us into who we had become over the years. Some of us spoke about the influence of attending youth groups as a young person. I can remember as a kid in middle school being drawn to attend youth group with all my Catholic friends. I have fond memories of eating pizza and going to the dances. It was a time in my life where

I felt like I belonged. The dances and food were the way the church engaged the youth, including those like me whose parents had fallen away from the Church. The youth would gather, and I'd listen to the prayers and watch all the beauty taking place in the Mass.

The Lord was shifting puzzle pieces around for the purpose of helping me to discover Him in a deep and lasting way. The summer after Isley died, I met a new mom, Shandie, one day while working out at the gym. Shandie was very easy to get along with, vibrant, and always smiling.

In October, Terri—Emma's former speech therapist—Courtney, a mutual friend, and Shandie all attended a Cursillo weekend together. That same weekend, my sister, Ashley, Misty, and I attended a woman's conference in Dallas. It was on this trip that I decided to sign up for RCIA so I could catch up on the sacraments I'd missed. I had been baptized, but my family stopped attending the Catholic Church before I could make my first Holy Communion.

When I met with Ms. Emmaline, our parish's RCIA director, she took inventory of where I was in my faith, and because I was open to the idea of Confession and desperately needed it, that's directly where she sent me. She suggested—ahem, more like ordered—I go have a face-to-face confession with our parish priest, Fr. McIntyre. Ms. Emmaline is beautiful in her gentle and loving wisdom.

At the time, I didn't understand the sacrament of Reconciliation and I didn't think I would get much out of it. To my surprise, when I left the confessional, I felt amazing, like a heavy burden had been lifted from my weary spirit. I couldn't see it, but I felt different. For the first time in a long time, I sensed a peace that had been buried under a big pile of trash. I envision that confession as Father literally helping me take out all my trash. No recycling, just throwing it all away.

Shandie and I were attending these RCIA classes at Ms. Emmaline's home because of our schedule. Shandie had not made her Confirmation, but was living out her faith and wanted to go deeper in her relationship with Christ.

In February of 2017, Shandie and I were Confirmed, along with the high school kids in our parish. That was a very humbling experience, to make your Confirmation with kids who have parents the same age as you. It was such a gift to be able to go through this with a friend, to have the support of a spiritual sister, and to have our larger group of spiritual sisters there supporting us. I cried, but this time it was happy tears.

This led me to the next step in my spiritual reawakening, which was gently encouraged—who am I kidding, I was pushed—by my spiritual sisters to attend my own Cursillo weekend. A much needed push. I regularly told them that I'd make my Cursillo one day, but I just wasn't ready to face my grief yet. My grief was the source of so many fears and anxiety that putting a carpet over the stain was the quickest way to not see the mess. Well, the time had finally come, and I felt ready. It was a promise I had made them, so I couldn't back out. I chose Shandie to be my Cursillo sponsor because we had been on the Confirmation journey since the summer before.

That weekend, which happened to be the weekend before the one-year anniversary of Isley's death, Shandie dropped me off at the Cursillo center in Prairie Ronde, LA. I could sense Isley and the twins with me there at the Cursillo center. Together in heaven, I felt them praying for me the entire time. I had so many signs that I had come at the right time. Had I gone sooner, I don't think I would have been transformed so radically.

From the outside, it may appear like my reversion was fast and drastic, but God had been working on me for seven years in subtle ways. He was such a gentleman, pursuing my broken, delicate heart. It was like God finally said to me, "Kelly, it's time" and removed my blinders.

I became a different person after my Cursillo weekend—someone I could love again. It was on that weekend that I accepted the invitation to walk with the Holy Spirit by visiting the sacraments multiple times, and it seemed each one broke down another wall I'd constructed around my heart. It wasn't until then that I was able to be totally free, totally and recklessly in love with Christ.

It may have taken me longer than others, but like the woman with the alabaster jar not caring about the cost of her gift, I, too, smashed my vessel and gave Him my all.

Chapter Fifteen

CALLED TO MINISTRY

"Christ has no body now but yours. No hands, no
feet on earth but yours. Yours are the eyes through
which he looks compassion on this world. Yours are
the feet with which he walks to do good. Yours are
the hands through which he blesses all the world."

—Teresa of Ávila

I WAS IN THE KITCHEN ONE SUNDAY COOKING A GUM-
bo as my husband and daughter sat on the back patio watching LSU
baseball. The weather had been stormy all afternoon. With nothing
much else to do, I decided to look around for a movie. I flipped
through the movie titles and came across *John Paul II* starring Jon
Voight, a movie I had wanted to watch for some time.

While watching the movie I learned a great deal about this saint's
early life, including the loss of both of his parents and family when
he was young. Even amid persecution, he desired to become a priest,
but with so much fighting in Poland, the bishops were not allowing

young men to enter the seminary. Instead, Karol Wojtyla joined the theater and ministered to the youth by becoming an underground youth minister. When it was permissible, he joined the seminary where he acted on his holy call to the priesthood and was ordained in November of 1946. Thirty-one years later, on October 16, 1978, Fr. Karol Wojtyla was elected to the papacy. October 16 is the day my twins were born.

As I continued to watch the movie, the love of St. John Paul the Great grew inside my heart. His was such a beautiful love story of a man after God's heart, and I marveled at the way the Holy Spirit was able to lead him through obstacles. His love spread throughout the world during his papacy.

He was known as the Pope of Families, and his desire to transform and restore our Church was a sight to witness. He was a holy man so in touch with the Sacred Heart of Christ that their two hearts united and poured out to the world, into the Church, and into our homes. A great saint had found me and attached himself to my prayer life. St. John Paul the Great stood by me as a role model for how God calls us all to love and serve our neighbors.

This call to love and serve our neighbors didn't exactly set off a light bulb for me to begin grief support ministry, but God was giving me pieces to digest over time. I am one of those people who needs a bunch of literal signs from God to be sure of His message. One usually isn't enough, and He has to give me a couple more. I've been fortunate to be aware of little signs He's putting in my path, like connecting numbers and dates that have significance. The Lord is always so patient and gentle with me and gives me the signs that I need, because He created me and knows the best way to reach me.

It's easy for me to miss things, not because I'm not bright, but because I'm a busy bee. I don't slow down often enough to watch the world. I don't often sit still long enough to hear the Lord. I have to force myself to be still and create a silent space to hear His voice. Because of my stubbornness, God has to speak to me in the midst of my busy schedule. Sometimes He would even wake me from sleep with a message.

The movie about St. John Paul the Great really caught my attention. God chose him to be pope on the same day He chose to appoint us Talon and Emma Grace's parents. When the movie ended, it was still raining and it was too early to go to bed, so I chose another movie. This is so out of the ordinary for me to have time to sit and watch movies, so I know that this time and the order that I watched these two movies was the Lord showing me the path He wanted to lead me down.

The second movie I watched that day was St. Teresa of Calcutta's movie *The Letters*. St. Teresa was a pillar to our modern-day church. Her piety and devotion to the sick was such a beautiful witness, but the story of how she was able to follow her "call within a call" was equally exquisite.

St. Teresa was the principal at a Catholic school in India, and from her second-story window she would watch the poor literally dying before her eyes. This moved St. Teresa and she felt convicted to help. She went to her Mother Superior several times, and Mother Superior kept telling her no, that she couldn't leave the convent to help the poor people in the streets, and would shoo her away.

After several failed attempts, Mother Superior told her to go on a retreat and when she got back, they would talk. St. Teresa boarded a train leaving Calcutta and it was on that train that she heard God's voice, what the Church has referred to as her "call within a call." The day St. Teresa boarded the train was September 10, the day Emma Grace was baptized and the day she died. When St. Teresa returned, she gained permission and left her convent, with nothing, to start the Missionaries of Charity in Calcutta.

I felt that St. John Paul the Great's movie was a leading from the Lord that confirmed a desire I'd been considering for some time, which was to start a youth ministry within our parish at St. Bernard. His connection to the youth sparked my connection to my parish, but it would take more time to discern my "call within a call."

You see, I was incredibly quiet and shy growing up, so to feel capable of what He was asking of me—doing ministry of any sort— would require me to do some growing up, spiritually and emotion- ally. I needed to face my fears and navigate my way through my own pain and weaknesses. I was still learning how to trust again and needed some guidance and more life experience to accomplish what He wanted me to do. I began learning all of the spiritual aspects of ministry by leading the youth in our parish. I realized a lot about myself during that time.

Fr. McIntyre allowed us to begin a middle-school ministry pro- gram called Edge. The youth ministry was a way to get me out of my comfort zone. I figured talking to kids in middle school had to be pretty easy; I mean, they're kids and don't really listen to what adults say anyway, right? If I said something stupid, they likely wouldn't hear me or care. I assumed that as long as I fed them pizza, played games with them, gave a twenty-minute talk about the faith, and then let them meet in small groups, they wouldn't judge my character or flaws. Easy peasy.

Wrong.

Well, the kids were great but it took me about six months before I felt comfortable in front of them. I was totally out of my element. Those beautiful young souls stretched me as much (or more) than I did them. The kids loved learning the truth about God and asked some heavy questions. But most of what stretched me was my inexperience with the material I needed to present. As a result, I had to prepare a lot in advance on nights when Edge met. I wanted to make each experience with Christ personal. It was important to me that the children have fun while learning and discover a love for their faith. I desired to become holier because of who they were, and who they needed me to be. And as time went by, I began to see all the ways God was healing my anxious heart.

Along with youth ministry, I was also drawing from the tools I learned about in Cursillo. I didn't realize that regularly participating in the sacraments could make a person feel fully alive. The grace alone filled me up and made me a new creature. Many people would comment that they noticed in me a peace that only is seen on the face of someone who has witnessed light shatter the darkness.

As the year progressed, I began to feel like the youth ministry was only the first part of what the Lord was calling me to. I loved what I was doing, but it didn't come naturally to me. I knew one thing really well, and that was how to survive the loss of a child. Not that I was good at it, but I could be my authentic self when sharing how God was present to me in my darkness. I didn't have to study grief, or take classes to know how to navigate those waters, all I had to do was reflect on my own story.

And then, on August 19, 2017, Ryan attended a men's conference during which he stepped into the confessional after being away from it for fifteen years. The celebrant who heard his confession was Fr. Brady.

Fr. Brady was so moved by Ryan's confession that he actually invited Ryan and me to share our story at his parish. We felt that maybe this was a sign from God that we could possibly help others on their grief journey, but when Fr. Brady gave Ryan his phone number and told him to give him a call, I procrastinated out of fear. I didn't know what being vulnerable with strangers would feel like, and I let that unknown freeze me in my tracks.

In hindsight, I see I still had some growing and discerning to do. I kept Fr. Brady's phone number for seven months. That invitation opened in me the idea that my story was worthy to be heard. I kept thinking about what it would be like to share my grief with other grieving couples. What if we started a ministry for grieving families? What would that look like? I asked myself so many questions, and I didn't have answers for any of them.

I thought about the grief support ministry often, but I still questioned if it was something I wanted to go through. Grief is exhausting and revisiting those wounds left me feeling like I was going backward. This was not the case, it just felt like it in the moment. We heal in layers, and sometimes to have true healing, we need to peel off the scabs and show the wounds to Him again.

After thinking about this for some time, I began to wonder if grief ministry was my "call within a call." I contemplated what was going on inside my heart so I could discern His will for me. His plan is perfect, not mine, but I was so confused about what He was asking of me. Easy to say, hard sometimes to accept when you know you have to release control. That, to me, was the scary part. I didn't know what was going to happen if I said yes.

About two months after the conference, a friend stopped me as I was leaving Mass. Her two daughters were in Edge, and she was helping lead one of the small groups. I told her about what had happened at the Man to Man Conference that Ryan had attended, and how Fr. Jim Brady asked him if we would be interested in giving a talk at his nearby parish about the loss of our twins.

My friend encouraged me to seriously think about it, but more importantly, she asked me to consider leading a grief support ministry at *our* parish. I had just been in Adoration praying about this desire He had placed on my heart. She'd already mentioned it to our parish priest, Fr. McIntyre, and he thought it would be a great idea for me to help those who had just lost a loved one. I did not initially think this was something I wanted to pursue. I was still navigating the waters and had just rediscovered the healing power of the sacraments. How would I even begin something so important?

I should have known right away, but sometimes those big lessons take time to sink in. I was listening to my inner voice, which was filling me with feelings of doubt, fear, and unworthiness. I've since learned how to determine whose voice I'm hearing in these situations. God always calls a person by name; the devil calls us by our sins. I didn't respond to Fr. Brady's request for Ryan and me to speak at his parish, and I didn't call Fr. McIntyre about leading a grief support ministry. There were just too many things to be afraid of that were holding my "yes" hostage.

Over the next seven months, God spoke to me in ways I couldn't deny. I went from knowing only one or two people who had experienced child loss to meeting dozens. It was like the Blessed Mother, God the Father, the Son, and the Holy Spirit were playing chess in heaven. I was one of those chess pieces, and they would move other pieces in my path, people He wanted me to meet who needed help.

The grieving person's little saint was petitioning God to move heaven and earth for me to meet their mom or dad. There is no other possible explanation but divine Providence. I imagined with each person I met and spoke with in this ministry, God would say "checkmate" to the enemy. If He wills it, His will will be done, one way or another. The communion of saints began to come alive for me. There was just no other explanation for how the parents of all of these little saints were finding me all over our community.

My not accepting the journey initially was all part of God's master plan, because He was building confidence in my ability to embrace my strength and unite it with Christ's strength. This grief journey has been hard, but God continues to use my healing as a way to stretch me into who He made me to be. I felt the Lord tugging deep at this idea of grief support for parents who have experienced child loss. God began to lay images in my mind of what this ministry could look like.

That day, seven months after the Man to Man Conference, I gathered my courage and called Fr. Brady. Of course, I would get his voicemail, and of course it would say he was on vacation for two weeks. I left a message, walked into my kitchen, and said out loud to

God, "What do You want me to do next?" I was suddenly overcome with a crystal-clear thought: *Find the yellow legal pad where you started writing this story.*

God will not bring you to something and then leave you. I found the notepad containing the beginning of my book that I'd started some six years earlier. I took it back into the kitchen, flipped to a blank page, and started writing. I believe God had me put the book down six years earlier because I wasn't in a place emotionally or spiritually to accomplish His will just yet.

I had stopped at the tomb. I was only looking at death through one lens, and Christ wanted me to travel all the way to Pentecost. I needed to trust that He would never leave me, that He would send his Advocate to be with me. He wasn't leaving me tied up to my pier. My sailboat, masked with a number of sails, wouldn't remain stuck in the harbor. I needed the Holy Spirit to fill me up so that I could move forward.

God did not create me to be a docked ship but one that sails the sea and travels the lands of child loss. He sent the love of His Son and the Holy Spirit to undo the knots in the rope that tied it to the pier. He released the sails and sent forth His breath into my sails, and I began to move forward.

I initially thought I'd begin writing my talk on grief so that when Fr. Brady returned my call, I would have some of it completed. Well, again, God smiled at my plan and then unleashed His. He filled my sails enough so that my movement wasn't just slow and steady; He moved me to feel His wind whip across my skin, and the words flew out of me. What was supposed to be just a talk came later, after I'd written the rough draft of this book. God had lead me through so much, and He wanted me to share it in its entirety.

While writing my book, God revealed some profound things to me. Some of the ideas actually made me question my sanity. Did I really hear that, God? Did You just answer me? Questions that unless you know the Father's heart, you would never think to ask.

One of the bold statements that I heard from God was to crush the Mary heresy. At the time, I didn't even know what a heresy was. I now know that heresy is a belief that contradicts religious doctrine. The truth was, I didn't fully understand Mary's role in the Church. I knew I had heard God's message clearly, but I didn't know why or how I was to speak on Mary's behalf to defend her role as Queen Mother.

As a reverted Catholic, my relationship with Mary has grown into something beautiful, but this wasn't always the case. I had all the same assumptions as the Protestants, thinking that Catholics worship Mary. Now I understand that what may look like worship is us honoring her for her perfect discipleship and for being obedient to God and saying yes even when the situation was scary. It also became a great comfort to me that, like me, Mary had to endure the pain of watching her Son suffer and die. She was a mother of child loss too.

I was nervous about how I was going to defend her to others, particularly grieving mothers who may be angry with God and won't want to hear about faith. But I knew that the heart of any grieving mother would relate to hers the most. I had to trust and do this for Him.

God showed me Mary. He said, "She is who you need to bring into the conversation." When I asked Him why and how, His response left me speechless. Standing in my foyer, tears streaming down my face, I heard Him say: "Because you are Mary."

I was confused. "God, if You want me to do this, I need to know more about what You mean." He asked me, "What was your biggest fear after Talon and Emma Grace died?" I responded, "That people would forget that they had been born and had lived." God asked me, "What is your role as Talon and Emma's mother now?" And I knew with certainty how to respond. "To make sure no one ever forgets them."

I imagined the look on God's face as kind and loving, but firm. God asked me, "What do you think Mary does for Jesus?" And that's when I finally understood. Mary, the mother of Jesus, does for Jesus what we do for the beloved children we lost. Like Mary, our role is to make sure our children are never forgotten. We get to Jesus through Mary.

Mary isn't looking to get the glory. She always points back to Jesus when we implore her. Her mother's heart finds us in our puddle of tears and gently lifts our chins and points us to her Son.

Without Mary, my journey would look so different. She has the same grieving heart and she reminds me that I can walk this journey with her to Him.

Around this time, a friend of mine said, "Kelly, God is leading you down a different path than you initially thought. Look at what He is revealing to you! How can you deny this? You should consider this grief support ministry. Don't just think about it, you need to discern if this is what God is calling you to do."

But I kept questioning myself. I couldn't imagine God would call me to this, but looking back, I see that the Lord has showed me things that I never otherwise could have known. Remember, I was not formed in the faith. I did not attend one day of CCD that I remember. I was not raised Catholic, and when I started writing this book, I was still relatively new to the Catholic faith.

But God would lay ideas on my heart, and then the next day or week, I would pick up a book or meditation and there would be the same or similar words that He'd given me. God was showing me that I didn't need some vast formation to know His Sacred Heart. I just needed to be open to His love, and reflect that love back.

He was going to reveal to me exactly what I needed to know, if I was willing to ask the hard questions. It had to be that He was revealing these important mysteries to me about His divinity because I've suffered so much. My heart needed to know these profound truths in order to see my heart, outside of my own body, healed. He knew that I would recklessly say yes to Him if I truly understood.

I learned on my Cursillo weekend that this profound transformation and reorientation of my life to God is called *metanoia*. Metanoia is a spiritual change of heart and can be traced back to the Gospel of Mark when Jesus announces that the kingdom of God is at hand and asks for repentance. "I do will it. Be made clean" (v. 1:41). The leper had the desire to be healed and had faith in Christ's ability to heal, but it wasn't until he asked that he was made clean. The key is to ask.

I started prayerfully considering leading a grief ministry. God gave me many encouragements during this time to know this was what He was calling me to, but I trace it all back to the day I learned about St. John Paul the Great and St. Teresa of Calcutta and the order of those two dates, as the proof that God was preparing me for this next journey, calling me out of the first call to receive the gift of the call within the call.

Like stained glass, He put me back together again piece by piece. He restored my faith, answered my questions, and helped me learn how to trust Him again. Now it was time.

The trust that I needed was shown to me over and over in relationships as well as within my own heart. Friendships within my church circle, but also friendships with saints that I embraced and leaned on for prayerful support.

Have you seen the photo of St. John Paul kissing the top of St. Teresa of Calcutta's head as she's holding his hand in hers? This picture sits in the foyer of my home, and I often find myself studying this embrace. How gentle and loving they held each other.

They were the man and woman of the century, who together made and changed history for all. They were pilgrims of peace, individuals who were deeply in love with God and neighbors, supporters of the poor and the marginalized, promoters of human freedom and human dignity. Saints on earth long before they died and were canonized.

St. John Paul the Great witnessed what he called the Mystery of Woman and the great works of God through the woman. He was the first pope to address a letter directly to women.

These two saints believed in the same goals of the apostolate and opened their arms wide for the Church and the people. They brought to the faith a sense of family and belonging. Their friendship was so deep and gentle. Through their great friendship, I realized just how much parents who have lost children need mercy and to feel this same embrace.

I was compelled to spend time in Adoration and give this desire of ministry to God, put it at His feet, and hear from Him what was next. In Adoration God revealed to me what this grief support program was to look like, and what He intended for me to create. Ten topics were laid out before me in a matter of minutes. This is such a delicate and much needed ministry, and He was shaping it through me.

I walked out of Adoration with a notebook full of notes and ideas, and who did I run in to but the very same friend who months before had encouraged me and told me God was calling me to something greater. She'd asked, "Are you going to embrace this ministry or are you going to just sit back and wait?" This is what "iron sharpening iron" looks like (Prov. 27:17).

I will always remember that on September 10, my inspiration came, not from a place of comfort, but of suffering. On that day, Jesus' thirst for love and for souls took hold of St. Teresa's heart, and the desire to satiate His thirst became the driving force of her life. Similarly, Emma Grace Breaux had been baptized and became God's beloved daughter on September 10, 2006, and passed away exactly three years later, on September 10, 2009.

Her death changed my life, and my first divine vocation of motherhood gave birth through my suffering to my next vocation, Red Bird Ministries.

Chapter Sixteen

WEDDING RE-BLESSING

"The path of holiness lived together as a couple is possible, beautiful, extraordinarily fruitful, and fundamental for the good of the family, the Church, and society."[7]

—St. John Paul the Great

WHEN I FINALLY MADE MY CONFESSION, CONFIRMAtion, and then Cursillo, I had this deep desire for Ryan and me to renew our marriage vows for our fifteenth wedding anniversary. On July 15, 2017, we renewed our vows in sanctifying grace, totally surrendering our marriage and our family to Christ again on the altar.

I cannot describe how amazing we both felt saying our vows to each other again, all these years later, crucified, wounded, beaten, broken, transformed, molded, and re-created again. I don't think I've

[7] From Encyclical: *Beatification of The Servants of God Luigi Beltrame Quattrocchi And Maria Corsini, Married Couple*, Homily of John Paul II, Sunday 21 October 2001, World Mission Sunday, paragraph 3

ever loved my husband more than I do today. It is possible for a marriage to thrive after child loss. The key is to make sure you are healing together.

Jesus, the Divine Physician, has miraculously healed us. The perfection we were striving for ages ago ceases to exist. We had placed so much effort in collecting material items and climbing social statuses, but after our conversion, we realized that those things are no longer necessary for happiness. Our peace was restored and reordered, and the anxiety that was constant got replaced by the grace and love from Our Father.

This grace that I was chasing, this peace that I desired, came through the sacraments, and renewing our vows proved to be one of those special healing moments that you notice only in hindsight. I often say that things only make sense backward. But what I realized is that faith means doing things blindly, and seeing the grace is the reward. This was exactly what happened.

My grief had clouded my judgment and had shaken my trust in God and other people. When people would suggest the obvious, like that we needed to go back to church, I would brush them off and think they had no idea what they were talking about. I wouldn't take advice from people who hadn't gone through what I'd gone through because I assumed they had no idea how to relate.

I'm ashamed to say I often wouldn't even give people a chance to offer suggestions or advice out of love for us. I was totally closed-minded. I couldn't see how they were genuinely trying to help me and wanted to love me though my loss. I see now that I was angry. Not with people, but with God.

In God's divine love and infinite wisdom, He showed me just

how much I knew about His love, which was not a whole lot. I thought that I was unloved and unlovable by the Father, but here He was performing miracles before my very eyes, not for His sake, but for mine. He knew just what I needed to see in order to believe. I was Thomas in every instance.

One of these moments happened during our anniversary trip the week after we renewed our vows. God came to me in a dream. God is known to have communicated with St. Joseph through dreams. For the record, I am no St. Joseph, or St. anybody for that matter, but I could relate to how real and powerful those dreams were to him, and how convicted he was to follow God.

Saturday, July 22, 2017, we boarded a plane to Antigua to celebrate our fifteenth wedding anniversary. I had been praying a novena to St. Anne for the opportunity to attend Mass in a third-world country. I was worried because I didn't want to put myself or Ryan in danger getting there. I should not have worried so much, but Estelle was nine, and she needed her mother and father to come back alive. I knew if I was prayerful and faithful to God, He would protect us.

When we boarded the plane in New Orleans, I got my Rosary out, as I always do at take-off, and began my prayers. While I was praying, I overheard a conversation between the man next to me and the girl in front of him. I shouldn't have been listening while I was praying, but I couldn't help myself; I'm nosy. They were talking about a mission trip they were headed to.

Curious, I asked where they were going and discovered the man was in fact a Jesuit priest. Because of my lack of catechism, and general lack of experience being a fully-engaged Catholic, my response was, "We are Roman Catholic." Can you imagine what this sweet

Father must have thought? I'm giggling as I write this because since then my knowledge and love of the faith has only grown, and in that moment of humility, I learned a thing or two from him. Sit still, stay quiet, and just pray.

Sitting there holding my Rosary, I felt the need to tell Father about my prayer request. I told him about my novena to St. Anne with special intentions that we would make it safely to Mass that Sunday. Father thought this was so beautiful how the desire of our hearts to not miss Mass was taken to prayer. I was convinced that this was a sign from God, but He had not finished telling me how He was answering this prayer.

After we wrapped up our conversation, a movie began. It was about a girl who would be going before a judge in order for her uncle to adopt her. The court date was on Emma and Talon's birthday. I viewed this as a special message from heaven, a sign God gives once we give it all to Him. But God did not stop there, He kept revealing to me just how much He was guiding our hearts and souls through this beautiful celebration of renewing and re-blessing our marriage in sanctifying grace. I needed to sit back and hold on. I had asked Him, petitioned in prayer, and in His own way, I was learning to trust that He would answer.

We arrived in Antiqua. The next morning, which was Sunday, we got a van to take us to the Cathedral for Mass. The date was July 23, the eight-year anniversary of Emma's final surgery.

I can remember walking into the Cathedral, and as I do every time I visit a new church, I mentally photographed the details inside. The tabernacle, the crucifix, the altar, all the beautiful sights and sweet smells. I do this as a way to elevate my prayers and my attention to God in the silence and prepare my heart for Him. It's the very place where God will come down from heaven and sweep us into His heavenly feast. I love to take in all of that beauty while I kneel to pray. I have a deep appreciation for all the ways Catholic Churches use our senses to worship God.

At the end of Mass, the priest asked all who were celebrating anniversaries to come up for a blessing. A lay person presented us with a special Rosary and Father blessed us with a special marriage blessing. The choir sang to us and loved on us in a way I haven't experienced before. It was so special, and I will never forget that day.

Three days later, on July 26—a date I'll always remember, because it was the last time I heard Emma tell me she loved me—God revealed to me my mission through a dream. As Emma had told me she loved me on that date, God also told me He loved me by revealing His divine plan for Ryan and me.

In the dream, I was being pulled through a gate, as though by an invisible cord, toward God. It wasn't a smooth pull, but a jerking, dragging-my-feet kind of pull. I wasn't fighting Him; I was just scared of what was happening. As I drew closer, He became vivid, and I could see His face, but not clearly.

He was magnificent, dressed in white and His hair was flowing as if the wind was blowing, but I didn't feel any wind. I knew who He was but the features of His face didn't have definition. They were blurry like an out-of-focus image you see at the ophthalmologist's office. The harder I tried to focus on His face, the harder it was to see Him with any clarity. He was just too bright to look at, like when you try looking at the sun. In the dream, my eyes started puddling tears.

His features appeared Middle Eastern, dark skin, and His shoulder-length hair was wavy and as white and pure as snow. His robe was iridescent and made of pure light. It seemed to be reflecting from a separate light source. The clouds floated on the ground like fog over the ocean waves, and I felt like I was walking toward Him on water.

He sat on this large golden-brushed throne, flanked by two adoring angels who faced Him. He had a staff in His right hand and was holding His left hand out to me, motioning me to continue forward.

I was nervous, shaking, trying to figure out why God would visit me again. I thought, *I am not worthy of this visit, Lord.* But before I could speak, He asked me if I would receive the gifts of the Holy Spirit. I thought about this and wanted to tell Him that I already had received them, at my Confirmation, but who was I to question God? There had to be a bigger reason for Him to ask me this again. I hesitated and then said yes.

Still confused, but trusting Him, I placed my hand in His hand, laid my head in His lap, and He began to stroke my hair, two or three times with the love only a Father has for His beloved daughter. And then I awoke.

The reason I know for sure that I was not just dreaming was because when I awoke, my hand was outstretched, and the warmth on my arm and hand felt like an embrace. Not like when you leave your arms out of the covers and they're cool to the touch. I laid in bed and cried until I fell back asleep, still questioning if that had really just happened.

I kept this dream to myself, contemplating its significance. Over the next few days and weeks, I wondered if I was superimposing the architecture of the Cathedral in Antiqua into my dream. The look of God's throne, the adoring angels . . . Then I realized, it matched the look of our church back home. Our tabernacle is gold and on two columns on either side of the tabernacle, angels are genuflecting, adoring and protecting God.

The more I thought about it, the more certain I was that God had truly spoken to me that night on July 26, in Antigua. He did indeed ask me if I truly wanted to receive the gifts of the Holy Spirit. I kept this dream in my heart only telling Ryan and my friend Courtney, unsure of its meaning, but trusting they would respect my privacy until one special day when I was ready to talk about it.

In October 2017, my friend Ashley and I decided to attend a retreat put on by the Dominican Sisters of Nashville, Tennessee. I drove to New Orleans and spent the night with her so that we could fly to Nashville the following morning.

When we landed, we decided to stop at the Dominican Motherhouse to see Sr. Mary Michael Fox. I had met Sr. Mary Michael at a women's morning meditation in Washington, Louisiana. Thanks to the Holy Spirit, we sat next to each other during the lunch talk. She spoke to my friends and me about the book we were reading, Venerable Archbishop Fulton Sheen's *World's First Love*. The book is about Our Lady, and Sr. Mary Michael was delighted that we were reading such a beautiful, eloquent book.

We ended our lunch asking Sister to pray for our group, and as she began praying, my tears hit the floor. It had been such a long time since someone had prayed so intensely and intentionally with me, touching the deepest parts of my heart. I will always treasure Sister's gift of loving me at a time when I was still so vulnerable and in need of prayer.

During this short visit, I was blessed with many signs from God that when we choose the path to heaven, the reward is an abundance of blessings. I surely saw Him in many encounters while I was present at the motherhouse.

When we were saying our goodbyes, I was prompted by the Holy Spirit to tell Sr. Mary Michael about my friend Molly, who had just recently loss her baby on the blessed Virgin Mary's birthday. I told Sister how the week before, I'd mustered up the courage to go and meet Molly for lunch, not really knowing her on a personal level, but only as acquaintances in our community.

Before our lunch, I went to a Catholic bookstore and carefully selected items that touched my heart to bring as a gift. I love bringing people gifts; it's just a way that I show my love. These gifts included a book, *Walking with Mary* by Dr. Edward Sri, a prayer card with Mary on it, a wall plaque of Mary and baby Jesus, and a card. Unbeknownst to me, Molly wasn't Catholic, and as she unwrapped the gift and told me about her faith, I was worried that she wouldn't want me there any longer.

But Molly was truly very precious and told me that through losing Everett, God had expanded her heart, and that she would indeed read the book, because she knew that I would never give her something that wouldn't help her heal. She needed a friend, and I was so blessed to get the opportunity to be a friend to another mom who had experienced child loss. Sharing this story with Sr. Mary Michael brought me to tears, of the power of receiving Christ's love through another.

Sr. Mary Michael, with her piercing blue eyes, grabbed ahold of my arms, the embrace was quick and scared me at first. She said, "God has anointed you, and this is your mission to lead others back to the Church. Be a light to others, especially those mothers who have experienced child loss, and lead them to Our Father."

She paused for a second and lowered her voice, "But you already know this, don't you?" Her words set me free, because I did know that but had fought accepting it time and time again—feeling brave, then cowering in fear. Saying yes to God, but then second-guessing my abilities. I needed something to really whop me upside my head for me to understand what God was clearly telling me.

It had to be God giving her this message otherwise how would she have known about the dream, the anointing of my head with the Holy Spirit, and the mission He had given me? I was speechless. She had uncovered something I knew was inside, and what I had believed to be true, but had sat on out of fear. I viewed the dream as an anointing, because the message was so clear to me. The gifts of the Holy Spirit were exactly what I needed to be able to fulfill His mission.[8]

God was calling me by my name and virtues, and Satan was calling me by my insecurities and my vices—my doubt, lack of trust, feelings of unworthiness, fear, self-pity, and selfishness. As I cried, unable to speak to Sr. Mary Michael, I just shook my head because I knew she was right. It was time I accepted my mission.

---

[8] The Seven Gifts of the Holy Spirit are Wisdom, Understanding, Counsel, Fortitude, Knowledge, Piety, and Fear of the Lord.

During this time of self-doubt, part of me was still scared and not sure if I could totally open my heart to be vulnerable with other grieving families. God was asking me to walk on water, with my heart opened wide, and only one of two things was going to happen. Either I was going to trust Him and fix my focus on His gaze, or I was going to sink.

After we left the motherhouse, I was unable to think about anything else as we drove the forty-five minutes to the Bethany retreat house. It was on this retreat where I discovered how God was equipping me for this very mission.

The retreat we attended was titled "A Walk with Our Lady" and was facilitated by Sr. Mary Madeline Todd, O.P., who currently is an assistant professor of theology at Aquinas College in Nashville. I had received an email about an upcoming women's retreat after signing up on their website. The retreat focused on how to walk with Our Lady through the mysteries of the Rosary. We walked through each mystery in a deep and profound way.

During the retreat, Sr. Mary Madeline's feminine genius was on point and every talk she led blew me away. "Feminine genius" is a term coined by St. John Paul the Great in 1995 in his pastoral letter titled "Letter to Women," which addressed the challenges of contemporary feminism. The letter offers a warning about forms of feminist ideology that are more destructive than constructive.[9] Sister beautifully connected the dots for us as she explained exactly what feminine genius was in light of Mary, our mother.

---

[9] John Paul II, "Letter of Pope John Paul II to Women" https://w2.vatican.va/content/john-paul-ii/en/letters/1995/documents/hf_jp-ii_let_29061995_women.html. Accessed 3/6/20.

It was a woman, the Blessed Mother, who said yes to God in her fiat. During the Annunciation, heaven invites Mary to receive Christ in her womb. The very place where love creates, and like Mary, all women are called to be a genius of receptivity: biologically, emotionally, and spiritually. A woman's body, like no man, has the ability to create a new life, but in order to be fully feminine, women's hearts and spirits must be receptive of this gift.

Walking with Mary during the retreat brought me into a closer relationship and understanding with Our Lady that I had desperately needed. Before the retreat, I had never understood how Mary's yes was not just a yes. God never uses anyone. In fact, because of her yes, He lifts us up above the angels, to be like Him.

This retreat turned out to be a highlight in my story, because I needed some motherly spiritual guidance, especially since burying my mom in 2015. I felt more alone in my journey without a mother figure worrying about my well-being. The Blessed Mother stepped into my life that weekend in a real and loving way.

A funny thing happened to me, a real lesson in humility. I didn't realize until we arrived at the motherhouse that this retreat was silent. They did not advertise that on the form, and I assumed that if it was to be silent, they would definitely have put that somewhere on the registration form or instructions.

I have always said that I would never attend a silent retreat because *I have to talk*. But I see now that the Lord sometimes forces us to get outside of our comfort zones in order to hear Him better. I can testify that I am someone who needs many, many loving pushes to get outside of my comfort zone. Who you see now is not the same woman who was shackled to her grief, but I have become a woman of redemption and fought through years of suffering to break the bondage of my fear and anxieties. Thanks be to God.

Sometimes the uncomfortable places will end up being a turning point of your grief. It was during this retreat that I heard Sister Mary Madeline Todd name the gifts of the Holy Spirit and realized they were the same words that God had spoken to me in the dream, asking me to receive them. Sister explained how God equips us for our mission by giving us these gifts, and I knew in that moment, when Sister Mary Michael said to me, "You have been anointed by God," that explained my dream and what God had revealed to me. He had given me exactly what I needed for the mission. I didn't need any special abilities or degrees. I needed only to be willing.

For such a long time, my heart and head were not in the same spot. My feelings of unworthiness, the depths of darkness where I had been during the lowest points, the visions of me on the floor as Ryan had to keep picking me up, they were all replaced with this white light, fearless and dangerous to the dark. I was ready to do God's will, not truly knowing what I was saying yes to, like Mary, but willing none the less.

He equipped me, He filled me up, and through a dream and advice from good friends, He made my mission known to me. A mission to help couples heal from losing a child or children. And how did He want me to do this? I was to show grieving couples God's love for them, point out all the ways that God was there for me even when I couldn't see or hear Him, and share with them my healing process by being transparent and vulnerable.

Chapter Seventeen

WHAT DEATH IS AND WHAT DEATH IS NOT

"Grief is the price we pay for love."

—Queen Elizabeth II

GK CHESTERTON WROTE THAT HUMAN SIGHT IS STEreoscopic: to view anything with only one eye is to see it wrongly.[10] If we focus on the struggle, or only on the cross we are carrying, and do not see beyond to the resurrection, we will remain in our grief for a long time. If we don't ever attempt to pick up our cross and run toward Christ, we will be missing out on so much help.

Our Lord desires to help us carry our crosses and even help others to carry theirs. We were never made to carry them alone. Think again of Simon of Cyrene, who helped carry Jesus' cross to Calvary. If we truly saw with both of our eyes, then we would see that through our crosses, we can witness our own resurrection. We run to help another grieving family carry their cross and in doing so, the love

---

[10] Gerard O'Shea, "A Vision of Education for Catholic Schools" *The Catechetical Review*, April–June 2018.

multiplies. This is what Divine Love does, it lays down one's life for a friend.

For years I couldn't see Christ's passion through my story. I guess I never felt worthy of having my story be compared in any way to what Christ did for us. But I think the resurrection gives us all hope that in our darkness, light can prevail. John 3:16 is a summary of Christ's salvation for mankind.[11] Our Salvation and transformation comes from the cross.

Death is never the end, but the beginning for those who believe. Physical death, although it may seem permanent, is not where our story fades out. If we live our life knowing that death is a gateway for rebirth, then we can find peace in death. As hard as it was for me to experience these losses, I now have peace in my heart. I imagine my babies in heaven with the Father, and I can smile picturing this. Knowing if I can't be with them, they have the love of the Father, the Son, the Holy Spirit, and the Blessed Mother loving on them until they welcome me into heaven's gates.

We've all been given the free will to choose to shine the light of Christ through ourselves and to see it in others, but sometimes it's hard to live that out when our grief consumes us and the darkness prevails. But we all have a choice. Will we remain in the dark, or will we choose to see the light? God doesn't force our response. He shows us the way to the light, and gives us the choice to follow or not.

It's been a long journey for us. It took time for me to choose light; I wanted to but it hurt so much to move on. When we live in the dark for so long, when we finally decide to turn on the light, it

---

[11] John 3:16 "For God so loved the world that he gave his only Son, that whoever believes in him should not perish but have eternal life."

hurts our eyes. We squint and tell the person who turned it on to turn it off. It sometimes is so painful that we cower and cover ourselves. But the only way we will ever adjust to the light in the room is if we turn it on and give ourselves time to adjust. If we choose to stay in the darkness because it's easier and because it doesn't hurt as much, we will get stuck there. Facing that light sometimes is too much to bear, but it's our only way to see the path that God is illuminating for us.

The simple fact of having to go on for Estelle forced me to turn on the light. In her innocence, I was reminded that she's worthy of having the best father and mother possible and this created a crack of light in my darkness. This beam of illumination hurt, but eventually I allowed it to shine.

Ryan and I were desperate to find a form of peace, because it gave us hope that one day we would resurrect, but we didn't know how or where to start. If we let Him, Christ will completely transform our hearts. The resurrection isn't about going back to life as normal, but coming through the other side of death glorified with Jesus, totally transformed and transfigured, seeing the glory of God and allowing His light to shine within us.

There were times when we tried our hardest to turn away from darkness and walk toward light independently, but we realized over time that it was impossible without Christ, and Satan knows this; that is why we can't face him alone. We need God; we need to call upon our Blessed Mother for her intercession; we need to call on all the angels and saints to come do battle for us. This is spiritual warfare, and our victory depends on who we have in our army. After the victory, the rest of the journey remains—a deeper, more profound conversion to become saints.

Those who survive a crisis without losing faith are often best able to be the bearer of hope to those who are suffering. If you have lost your faith and feel hopeless, please don't give up. I am living proof, through the darkness, God kept cracking my shell to shine rays of light on me. This is true whether it is a physical suffering or spiritual suffering.

Jesus' light transforms us so we may live in a way that is pleasing to Him. He reflects His light within us and it illuminates throughout the world. "Consider it pure joy, my brothers and sisters, whenever you face trials of many kinds, because you know that the testing of your faith produces perseverance. Let perseverance finish its work so that you may be mature and complete, not lacking anything" (James 1:2–4, NIV).

I became overwhelmed by compassion for those facing our same challenges. My desire to reach out and help others overcame me. I wanted to be the friend to those grieving mothers that I hadn't had when I went through my losses, someone who had lived through it and came out on the other side. I'd faced the same battle, and I had survived. I was, little by little, overcoming the darkness. Having this kind of support can be life changing for a family. My desire to show support to other families who were waking up to the same devastating news changed me. Love is stronger that death, and that enemy called death was defeated on the cross.

We believe and yet we can't see. This is what it means to look through only one eye, because the closer I get to Christ, the more I'm able to see. He has opened my eyes and lifted my veil. I see for the first time in a long time the beautiful and mystical body of Christ. I see the good in all that is visible, and I feel the warmth of Christ's embrace.

You must pursue Christ to feel Him, you have to be silent to hear Him, and you have to be opened to love Him and to let Him love you. Let your heart be like a monstrance in the morning, that places God in the forefront for the whole world to see. Go about your day with His love facing the world. Allow yourself to witness all the good that there is to witness, and at the end of the day, look at all of the beauty that is still present in your life. Then close that monstrance and start to pray. Pray in thanksgiving, and offer all of your daily works, joys, and gifts that He sent you that day, offer Him your heart.

The Catechism of the Catholic Church states, "Christ, Jesus the Son of God, transforms death, also he suffered the death that is part of the human condition. Yet, despite his anguish as he faced death, he accepted it in an act of complete and free submission to his Father's will. The obedience of Jesus has transformed the curse of death into a blessing" (1009).

What are we waiting for? What's holding us back? Jesus is asking us to walk on water, to have undeniable faith, to trust in Him completely and surrender all. In surrendering, the graces will pour out like the blood and water that poured out of His heart of divine mercy. "O Blood and Water, which gushed forth from the Heart of Jesus, as a fount of mercy for us, I trust in You."[12]

---

[12] Maria Faustina Kowalska, *Diary of Saint Faustina Kowalska*, public domain, entry 84; cf. 309

"You received without pay, give without pay" (Matt. 10:8).

How will you respond? Will you choose to measure the waves and watch them crash down upon the shore waiting for the perfect time to immerse yourself in your baptismal waters? Or will you take His hand, totally trusting that He will calm the storm and make walking on water possible? It's your decision.

The Venerable Fulton Sheen wrote, "When a child is given to his parents, a crown is made for that child in Heaven, and woe to the parents who raise a child without consciousness of that eternal crown!"[13]

I think a lot about these words and ask myself often, how did I prepare my twins for heaven, and am I preparing Estelle for heaven? It punches me in the gut some days. I think the reason I get so worked up over it is because I've had to think of this reality long and hard. For the twins, because they were not at an age of reason, I took comfort in knowing they went directly into heaven, but Estelle is of age. I'm constantly thinking of ways to help her with this journey and lead her closer to Christ's Sacred Heart. I want to see all of my children in heaven when it's time.

In today's day and age, we are living in, as St. Pope John Paul II states, "a culture of death." How can we raise little saints to run around the earth to evangelize and change the world? It starts at home, and it is our job to help lead our children to holiness.

I try my hardest to parent by the cross. We should live each day with the awareness that we aren't promised tomorrow, but not to fear, because death was defeated on the cross. We are not to live in

---

[13] Fulton J. Sheen, *Life Is Worth Living* (San Francisco, CA, Ignatius Press), 1999.

a state of mind that death of body or self is a bad thing, but just the beginning of our eternal life.

Having a Marian view of the cross has opened my eyes to what is most important in life. It has given my identity, rooted in Christ, a new meaning and a new understanding as a mother—a divine vocation given to me by God Himself. It has given me courage to go beyond the normal worries of motherhood, especially after loss, and trust Him with Estelle's life.

What we do as parents is live the faith to its fullest and act as a living testimony, a true witness to Christ. That, my friends, is exactly where we can say our divine vocation as wife, mother, and beloved daughter reflects the most beautiful gospel that Christ has written across our souls.

Now it's time to live it.

Chapter Eighteen

THE SACRAMENTS

"I have heard your prayer, I have seen your tears; behold, I will heal you."

—2 Kings 20:5

OUR TRANSFORMATION IN CHRIST CAN BE COMPARED to the winemaking process. First, the grapes have to be crushed, mashed down, and walked over; fermentation is basically the process of rotting. We all have to learn to die to self, like the grape. Once the grape has died, it can be transformed into something even better.

I confess, I didn't entirely understand the Eucharist before my reversion. I may have been able to say something about transubstantiation, but if I'm honest, my mind would go to those places of doubt and wonder if what we were doing as Catholics was what Jesus had intended. Now, when doubt creeps in, I remind myself to go read John 6:22–59, the Bread of Life Discourse, paying close attention to verse 54.[14]

---

[14] "Whoever eats my flesh and drinks my blood has eternal life, and I will raise him on the last day."

As hard as the teaching may be, we must trust our Church and our faith, or woe to those who turn their backs on the Eucharist and leave like the disciples did, returning to their former way of life. The Eucharist is transforming because it's Jesus' Body, Blood, Soul, and Divinity. He transforms us through His sacrifice, and we have the honor to taste His sweetness.

Through Reconciliation and the Eucharist, we get the chance to be purified, to lay all of our fears, worries, and grief at His feet. We can fall into His arms and let Him hold us through this dark night.

The Father knows what it is like to watch your child die. He watched Jesus die; He allowed Jesus to be crucified. Unlike us, He had the ability to save His Son, remove Him from the cross, unblemished, but He chose to allow Him to die to save all of us.

When we understand our Catholic faith, we can see what has been present all along. Allow your grief to open your heart, and once opened, make it a door for God to enter. Give Him the key. Our grief stretches our human mind and heart to further understand the mystery of God. As biblical scholar Jeff Cavins says in his You Tube video *Journey Home*, "Suffering is the lens through which we have ability to see 20/20."

There is a difference between doubt and difficulty. As the great Blessed Cardinal John Henry Newman wrote, "Ten thousand difficulties do not make one doubt, as I understand the subject; difficulty and doubt are incommensurate."

God allowed me to ask Him "why" until I was ready to hear His answer. The word *gift* never registered within me to mean my children. But eventually I came to understand the true meaning of the word *gift*.

During my suffering, God gave me three gifts: He strengthened me, He clarified my beliefs, and He helped me to understand the Gospel with compassion. This all equipped me to continue my own healing.

There will come a time when you will hit rock bottom and at that point, you must decide if you trust Him enough to give Him the chance to mend your heart. When you feel like your heart is mended even in the slightest, run toward God and don't ever stop running. Run as fast as you can.

Don't ever think you can do this by yourself. I wasted seven years trying, and like a hamster on a wheel, I got nowhere. A partial surrender won't work. He tore down my walls brick by brick, and I was transformed because I have seen the Father, and He has healed me.

Sacrament after sacrament, I realized that God was purifying me of my grief. I was being purged and healed. I was growing stronger the more time I spent in front of the Blessed Sacrament, in deep prayer and reflection. I was coming alive again. Feeling God in the presence of the sacraments is like sitting next to my best friend. But even better because my best friend has the ability and the desire to heal me.

I began researching and studying more about the Upper Room, the room where the Last Supper took place and where the disciples gathered after the Crucifixion. Everything I read was proof that my healing had come through the sacraments. One thing that surprised me was reading how four of the seven sacraments were instituted in the Upper Room.

Where I was hiding was the exact place where God met me! In my darkness, Jesus came through the walls, offered me peace, gave me what I needed to believe and receive, and He breathed new life into me.

I had been hiding in fear and had refused to surrender. The reason I was able to come out of the Upper Room and face my grief was because I allowed God to come inside and, being the gentleman He is, He simply offered me His peace, and I accepted.

The Lord exposed His wounds so that I would be comfortable showing Him mine. My wounds were cleansed by His when I celebrated my Reconciliation. Then the Holy Spirit descended upon me and anointed me with oil during Confirmation, and I was finally free and able to accept the mission asked of me.

This was how He showed me His glory and will for my life, a plan He knew before I was born. In accepting His plan, I was transformed and able to walk out of the Upper Room and into the world.

Chapter Nineteen

MAKING FRIENDS WITH THE SAINTS

"The most beautiful people we have known are those who have known defeat, known suffering, known struggle, known loss, and have found their way out of the depths. These persons have an appreciation, a sensitivity, and an understanding of life that fills them with compassion, gentleness, and a deep loving concern. Beautiful people do not just happen."

—Elisabeth Kubler-Ross, author of
Death: The Final Stage of Growth[15]

I EXPERIENCED A TRANSFORMATION IN THE UPPER Room, and I was ready to radically follow Christ. Like Mary Magdalene, I was ordinary but desired to be extraordinary. I wanted to give it all to God. Archbishop Roche once referred to her as "the Apostle of the Apostles." We know that Jesus had healed her after a personal

---

[15] Elizabeth Kubler-Ross, *Death: The Final Stage of Growth* (Prentice-Hall) 1975.

encounter. She had been possessed by seven demons, which He exorcised (Luke 8:1–3).

I often connect Mary Magdalene having seven demons attached to her soul—living in total darkness—to my grief, the dark space I was in after losing the twins. Many believe the number seven represents completeness, one reason for their being seven days in the week. But for me, the number seven, like her seven demons, represented my complete darkness. It was confirmation that my grief had consumed me entirely.

As I mentioned earlier in the book, I saw the world in color before the twins' deaths, and then my grief shadowed the world in grayness. Like Mary Magdalene, Jesus rescued me from the darkness, and my life had color again. The light prevailed, and I became the diamond that God created me to be, reflecting His love onto others like a prism. We say *De Colores* in Cursillo as a way of greeting to other Cursillistas. The phrase comes from this colorful prism—"the colors"—that reflects God's love for us while we reflect His love onto others.

Living my life in color, I saw how my heart, like the alabaster jar, had been broken and transformed into something greater. It wasn't until later that I realized, while reading a passage about the sacraments, that it had been them—a cumulative affect from my baptism, Confirmation, Reconciliation, and Holy Communion, consuming the body and blood of Christ in the Eucharist—that I had been healed. Even having our wedding vows re-blessed was celebrating again the sacrament of our marriage.

Transformation isn't a one-and-done event, but by regularly celebrating the sacraments, you progressively grow in sanctifying grace.

And that is life-changing. I had been telling people that I felt my true healing begin on my Cursillo weekend. During the three-day retreat, participants have daily Mass and Confession available to them. But the healing that I underwent isn't something that occurs over a single weekend. My reversion back into the faith was the result of several key experiences.

When I began RCIA, I was instructed to have a face-to-face confession with a deep examination of conscience. I scheduled time with my priest and we went through the list of sins; I was able to ask questions that had been weighing heavy on my heart, and Fr. McIntyre gently guided me through my anger and suffering. He gave me advice on God's Divine Mercy, something I wasn't familiar with or had ever felt. Divine Mercy is a devotion to Jesus Christ associated with the private revelations of Jesus to St. Faustina.

The message He gave her was simple: God loves us, all of us, and He wants us to recognize that His mercy is greater than our sins, so we can call upon Him with trust. In surrendering and receiving His mercy, it flows through us.[16]

After receiving the Eucharist in a state of grace, I made my Confirmation and renewed my baptismal promises. During my Cursillo weekend, I walked with the Holy Spirit like I never had before. It was there that I learned the tools I needed to walk with virtue, and I felt an intimacy with God that I had been missing for a long, long time. Walking out of the Cursillo center, I experienced for the first-time true sanctifying grace. I felt the light of Christ burning deep within my soul.

According to the *Catechism of the Catholic Church*, "Sanctifying

---

[16] Faustina, *Diary.*

grace is a habitual gift, a stable and supernatural disposition that perfects the soul itself to enable it to live with God, to act by his love, habitual grace, the permanent disposition to live and act in keeping with God's call, is distinguished from actual graces which refer to God's interventions, whether at the beginning of conversion or in the course of the work of sanctification" (*CCC* 2000).

I went to my Cursillo weekend broken, but partially put back together. My broken was invisible. You probably never would have pointed me out of the crowd as being the one who needed to be fixed because I masked my brokenness behind a smile. But so many times, God made it clear why I was there.

On my Cursillo weekend, one of the first signs that reinforced that I was where God wanted me was the table I was assigned to. Each table at the retreat is named after a saint. I was seated at the table of Mary Magdalene. The more I learned about her life, the more I felt like she chose me. Her life had been difficult and for years she walked in darkness. After she encountered Christ, He shattered her darkness. Through her healing, Jesus radically released her from all of her sins. She was healed, and He set her free. After that, she was on fire.

For Mary Magdalene and so many others who met Jesus during His three years of public ministry, the moment they met Him, they were transformed, and afterward they just couldn't sit still any longer. *They had to proclaim the Gospel!* Not everyone who met Jesus remained faithful to Him, but Mary Magdalene remained with Him until the very end.

One of Christ's most daunting, profound sorrows was that His close friends left Him in the final week of His life. I can relate to the feeling of abandonment. I needed people to understand how I was feeling, but to understand, you would have had to lose a child—and I didn't want anyone to know this pain. It was a quandary I felt stuck in.

Friends and family wanted their sister, daughter, and friend back, and I just wanted to be understood and given permission to grieve. I couldn't look beyond my grief and as a result, sometimes I hurt my family and friends, not because I wanted to, but because I was hurting and didn't know what to do. The hurt is overwhelming. Unfortunately, I wasn't able to always see or thank the ones who remained by my side, because I was blinded by the fog of my grief. For this I am truly sorry.

Jesus' friends abandoned Him when He needed them the most, in His final hours on the cross. A few of them, though, stayed to the end—His mother Mary; the apostle John; and Mary Magdalene (John 19:25). But Jesus forgave instantly, and His love is etched on my heart.

Mary Magdalene's compassion stretched out on the other side of the cross, to the tomb, during the pangs of grief, and through the resurrection. We should all desire to have friends as faithful as Mary Magdalene. What she showed me through her amazing faithfulness is to never give up on the people you love, because through prayer and faith, you will see their resurrection, and they will be glorified through Christ. Keep praying for those who suffer, keep inviting them to follow Christ, and be the light in the world of darkness that they so desperately need to see.

Mary Magdalene's love of Christ was extraordinary. This love drew her to see Christ in the tomb. I don't visit the cemetery very often because it isn't a source of comfort for me. I prefer to talk to Talon and Emma wherever I am when I feel the need to. But when I do visit, usually around the holidays, I watch families gather around their loved one's tomb. It's clear that their love for whoever died is so great that even in death, it's natural to be drawn to be with them, speak to them, and gather in remembrance.

Christ showed Mary Magdalene special favor and mercy for seeking Him through her suffering, and we see the special ways He rewarded her faithfulness after her conversion. Jesus rewarded Mary Magdalene with two gifts: He gave her the grace to remain in the suffering at the foot of the cross. And her love for Christ led her all the way to the tomb, where she was the first witness to Jesus' resurrection.

With these two experiences, her servant's heart received great rewards from heaven. Jesus chose Mary Magdalene; He honored her loyalty and faithfulness. A true servant has a willingness to serve beyond his or her capabilities, and a servant knows how to hear the Lord's voice. "For the Son of man also came not to be served but to serve, and to give his life as a ransom for many" (Mark 10:45).

This transformation set Mary Magdalene's heart on fire and inspired her to go out and proclaim the Gospel. She was freely given to and freely she chose to give. One of my deepest intentions in writing this book is for you, dear reader, to have an authentic encounter with Christ, and for your heart to be touched more intimately through a friendship with Him. He desires to heal you, but you must allow Him to. Follow the hemorrhaging woman's actions and reach forward in faith to touch the hem of His garment (Mark 5:25–34).

St. Thérèse of Lisieux, "The Little Flower," in her simple way, wrote of Mary Magdalene in her autobiography *Story of a Soul.*

> Yet most of all, I follow the example of Mary Magdalene, my heart captivated by her astonishing, or rather loving audacity, which so won the heart of Jesus . . . I have heard what He said to Mary Magdalene, to the woman taken in adultery, and to the Samaritan woman. No one can be frightened anymore, because I know what to believe about His mercy and His love; I know that, in the twinkling of an eye, all those thousands of sins would be consumed as a drop of water cast into a blazing fire.[17]

Over the years, at many times, it seemed there was no other way for me to survive than to fall into Jesus' arms. But I didn't always allow Him to catch me. I was so angry with Jesus and the decision I thought He had made for me. And on those days when I chose not to fall into His arms, I would hit the floor with a resounding thud. Even on those days when the floor would catch me instead of Jesus, it was a wake-up call. A blessing in disguise. *Why am I doing this to myself? It's not even productive, and it's not working. This feels like insanity.*

In the earlier days, when I chose not to let Jesus catch me, it was painful. But somehow, I would get back up, dust myself off, wipe the mascara tracks off of my face, and try again. Talk about willpower. Honestly, I don't know how I was able to do it other than God's

---

[17] St. Thérèse of Lisieux, *Story of a Soul*, the autobiography of St. Thérèse of Lisieux, (North Carolina, Tan Books, 2010), 154.

grace. God gave me grace I didn't deserve, but because He loved me so much, He gave it to me anyway. Now that's love.

St. Thérèse of Lisieux often wrote about how fragile she felt—small, weak, a crybaby most days. This was my life most days before I allowed God into my heart. While reading her autobiography, her humility and honesty sparked in me a deep devotion to this little saint. Her love of Christ magnified her weakness, and instead of Christ refusing this fragile flower, He delicately pruned her into a robust bloom of the most vivid color. She became a Doctor of the Church and reading about her life gave me great hope.

St. Teresa of Calcutta said it this way: "This is the perfect will of God for us: You must be holy. Holiness is the greatest gift that God can give us because for that reason he created us. Sanctity is a simple duty for you and me. I have to be a saint in my way and you in yours."[18]

---

[18] David Scott, *The Love that Made Mother Teresa* (New Hampshire, Sophia Institute Press, 2016).

Chapter Twenty

WALKING WITH MARY

"Even while living in the world, the heart of Mary was so filled with Motherly tenderness and compassion for men that no one ever suffered so much for their own pains, as Mary suffered for the pains of her children."

—St. Jerome

HAVE YOU EVER PICKED UP A ROSARY AND ASKED yourself why bother? I can remember how hard it was for me to understand why Mary was so important to the Church. This struggle was real, but I kept those feelings hidden in my heart. I didn't allow my doubt to cross my lips.

It was hard for me to fully comprehend my Catholic faith because I didn't understand Mary. The practice of saying the Rosary was something I did at funerals, so after my reversion, I did not pray it because it reminded me of my grief.

However, the more I studied my faith, and the more I reflected on Scripture and looked at my life, I formed a deep connection with her because we had maternal suffering in common. Thanks to the Holy Spirit, this revelation came in the form of a conversation that went something like this:

Jesus: Why don't you want to get to know My mother?

Me: Well, because I don't know her.

Jesus: You need to know her. I chose her, and I chose you to be Talon and Emma's mother. You know what a privilege the title of mother is. You know how important your children were to you. Do you think that Mary didn't love Me the same? Do you think that she didn't teach Me about My Father as you taught Emma and Estelle about Our Father? My mother?

Me: Jesus, I want to know her. I want to understand her. Please show me the way.

Over the years of my grief, I desired to learn more about Mary and to understand her through the eyes of Jesus. I knew that if I wanted to know her, that I would have to trust that He would give me many opportunities to do so.

Many times, in my search to know her better, Jesus would lay material out for me to contemplate: a book or a prayer. Other times it would be an encounter at a retreat or during time in Adoration. If you trust Christ, He will show you the way. The retreat "A Walk with Mary" at the Bethany House outside of Nashville was just the way He showed me.

Many of the Sister's talks focused on the mysteries of the Rosary, and what I learned led me into a deeper relationship with the Blessed Mother.

WALKING WITH MARY IN JOY

Learning about the mystery of joy, I was able to understand the simple path of Mary's fiat and what it meant when she said yes to the angel Gabriel. Our yes is a yes to do God's will. St. John Paul the Great said it well. "From Mary we learn to surrender to God's will in all things. From Mary we learn to trust even when all hope seems gone. From Mary we learn to love Christ her son and the Son of God."[19]

She expresses what was the fundamental attitude of her life: her faith. Mary believed! Mary trusted in His promises, and she chose life. Mary was open to the gift of life. A friend once told me to be open to life is to be open to death, but I wasn't open to the latter. The Blessed Mother shows us how to be open to God's will even when it involves death and loss. We have the ability to say yes to life, but unlike Mary, I wasn't open to accepting God's will. I struggled with the ability to trust in His goodness.

When God created woman, He created woman to bear a child. We have the space inside us for another, our womb. It is an act of total love to be able to conceive a child and give that child the gift of life that our Father has given to us. Mary shows us that her identity was the beloved daughter of a good Father, and her fiat was her trust in His goodness.

He provided her the surprise of a child and chose her specifically to embrace the Son of God inside her womb. Just like He chose me to embrace Talon and Emma Grace—even to the tomb, I was chosen. But I didn't believe in this calling because I wasn't open to

---

[19] Homily of His Holiness John Paul II at the Cathedral of Matthew, Saturday October 6, 1979, Washington, D.C.

death. I needed Our Lady's help to understand how to be open to God's will for my life.

Jesus loved His mother, and we should entrust our human struggles to Mary and let the Lord speak to us the words of truth and love as He spoke to her. She was given to us as a model in our pilgrimage of faith. Mary shows us how to say yes even with apprehension and confusion. She is the best example for being a disciple of Christ. Look to Mary to understand how to be faithful and to trust in God's word.

After listening to the talk on the mystery of joy, I spent some time in Adoration, meditating on what Sr. Mary Michael had said about me being anointed. I felt God was telling me to keep saying yes to Him, how my yes would lead many people to me that I would then be able to lead to Him. He told me that I was worthy of this calling, that I had suffered greatly, and not to doubt Him. He asked me to unite my pain and suffering to the cross and He would resurrect and transfix me. Transformed and lifted up by His name.

He asked me to let others know who He is, that He is a Good Father. Child loss doesn't feel good, so He needed someone to speak truth to the pain. He desired for me to bring those who needed healing to Him, and He would heal them, the brokenhearted (Ps. 147:3). He also instructed me to unite myself with Mary, allow her to grab my hand, and she would walk with me to Him, His Most Sacred Heart.

I heard the words that God spoke to my heart, and I wanted to say yes to each of His requests, but I didn't know or understand yet how this would be possible. I needed His grace. So I prayed, asking

Him to please make my heart a Eucharistic Heart.[20] A heart that could model His love for grieving parents. Surrendering myself entirely to Him was new to me, but I desired to do it.

That night at dinner we were allowed to take a break from our silence and talk amongst our table members. I sat next to a lady I will call Melissa. While we were talking, she told me about her son who'd had a traumatic brain injury a while ago, and three weeks before the retreat, he was given a communicator so that he could speak to his parents. With a big smile and glee in her eyes, she told us his first words. "I love you, stay with me." I was amazed because I'd read that those were the very same words St. Padre Pio would say after he received the Eucharist. I had adopted that practice when I received communion as well. I shared this with her.

Melissa started to tear up and told me that a few weeks before Jack received his communicator, some men from her church had brought St. Padre Pio's relics to pray with Jack. They offered a prayer for healing. My mouth fell open in shock. Christ used me to relay this information to Melissa. She was a mother grieving the life her son once had and yearning for Jesus to heal him. She needed to know that her son's prayers were heard. What a blessing to be able to witness that simple gift of self to this sweet lady.

The Lord works in many ways when you stay close to Him, and He allows you to bring Christ to others. "Abide in me, and I in you" (John 15:4).

---

[20] Having a Eucharistic Heart is a term I first heard at Cursillo. It is the model of love described by St. Paul in 1 Corinthians 13. Love is the source of the Divine Heart of Jesus, His Divine Love of each of us.

WALKING WITH MARY IN LIGHT

The next part of the walk focused on the Luminous Mysteries of the Rosary, something I was more familiar with as I had meditated on these while praying my Rosary at my weekly Holy Hour.

Mary always pondered the goodness of God, and her source of joy came from her Son and being His mother. We all can admit that our fullness of joy most days is our children. Walking with Mary keeps us close to living sacramentally. Frequently celebrating the sacraments will fill us with sanctifying grace. Mary, Scripture tells us, was "full of grace" (Luke 1:28). To be like Mary and walk in grace, we must walk a sacramental life.

Mary spent years taking care of Jesus, teaching Him the Hebrew Scriptures and how to pray the psalms. We can assume they spent a big part of their day-to-day life doing basic family chores like cooking and cleaning.

Today, it's easy to miss the sanctity in living a simple life within our family home. Having little ones limits our time with Jesus in the Eucharist as it's difficult to attend Mass as often as we want to, but the Sisters reminded us at the retreat that we can utilize the time we do have to pray while we are doing household chores. This is something I do often now when I really want to be in Adoration, but I'm needed at home with my family.

When Mary brought Jesus to the temple for circumcision, Simeon prophesized Jesus' Crucifixion and told Mary, "Your son will be a sign of contradiction and the sword will pierce your own heart" (Luke 2:35). Yet Mary continued to say yes to God even with the foreshadowing of the challenges her son would face. This was one of many yeses Mary gave to God. Part of my healing was learning how to say yes.

If you knew your child was going to die, would you continue down the same path you were on, or would you seek a new path? Personally, there is no way I would allow my child to suffer. I could never allow someone to murder my child.

Fortunately, God doesn't ask this of us. He did not create us for this mission, although my husband and I have carried much heavier crosses than the larger population of the world. God didn't ask us to sacrifice our child.

As hard as it was, Mary aligned her own will with that of the Father's. Imagine how pure and faithful Mary had been to be able to carry, raise, and love our Lord. Mary didn't stray from her path, she remained on course, even though the road would lead to the cross.

Her ability to say yes knowing the road would be hard helps me to understand how our desires and our plans can be very different from what Christ has planned for us. If Mary would have attached herself to Christ and not have accepted His will, then the story may have been quite different.

As author Kevin Carroll wrote in *A Moment's Pause for Gratitude*, "If we look into our hearts, and try to understand why a tragedy happens, but from a place of love, we may be able to see what God is revealing. Change your stinking thinking, and replace despair with gratitude. Gratitude changes everything." [21]

God's will for us is complete (Eph. 1:23). He doesn't come to destroy but to give us life in abundance (John 10:10) St. Ignatius of Loyola said it best: "God cannot be outdone in generosity" (2 Cor.

---

[21] Kevin Carroll, *A Moment's Pause for Gratitude* (California, BalboaPress, 2017).

9:8). No matter what we give back to God, it's His anyway. Our acceptance is not for His sake, but for our understanding of how much He loves us. He desires for us to know how much we are loved and worthy of all His blessings.

Living my life as a bereaved mother, I can honestly tell you that I would never be able to stay at the foot of my cross like Mary did. This road to healing requires total surrender and total trust. It's a daily decision. Some days, although I want to be healed, I still struggle to trust that He will heal me. I give it to Him and then I take it back, though I don't want to. It's a fight. I can admit that sometimes I tango with Jesus. I'm not always a good follower; I sometimes try to lead, but He loves me anyway. I think when I step on His feet, He giggles and then takes over and shows me how.

Mary, help me to be more like you. I pray that others will see your divine grace as the one and only chosen mother of our Lord and Savior. Blessed Mother, teach us how to love Jesus the way you do—unconditionally and totally—and help us cling to our cross and run toward your Son.

WALKING WITH MARY IN SORROW

This session was the hardest for me to walk through, but resulted in a great deal of healing. I saw for the first time the story of my life as a passion of sorts.

At the Bethany House retreat, Sister opened this session telling us that we weren't made to suffer. God created us in His likeness to share in His love. We were made to belong to Him, but sin separates us from Him. Suffering came into the world through original sin. But God's mercy and love is far more powerful than our minds can ever grasp. He can transform our suffering, if we let Him.

How are we saying yes to God when He asks us to accept a suffering? For me, it was extremely difficult. I didn't want to face my cross. I turned my back on my grief and my suffering to protect myself from the pain. I didn't want to even talk about it. You know you're nearing the last stage of grief when you are able to accept what happened and talk about the death of your child. I was so far for so long, but over time, especially walking with Our Lady, I slowly became ready and willing.

When Emma Grace died, I kept myself in denial, thinking, *This isn't my story. I must be in a nightmare I can't wake up from.* But as time passed, I began to understand my faith more completely. So many times I referred back to my fiat, the time when God asked me in a dream if I wanted my twins, even knowing the short time I would have with them. It became clear to me: accepting my situation and surrendering to God was the first step to my healing.

In the Annunciation, the archangel Gabriel announces to the Virgin Mary that she would become the mother of Jesus Christ. We have the opportunity to be like both Mary and Gabriel. We have the chance to hear God's message of love and promise to us, and then decide if we want to love back or to leave.

We speak on God's behalf, like Gabriel, when we share our story with other grieving parents. Sharing offers a light of hope. Sharing and listening are ways we can love these parents through their loss.

Despite their struggles, grieving parents are beautiful through and through.

We may struggle with our calling, especially since it is rooted in the loss of our children. We will wrestle with carrying this cross, like Jesus did when Simon of Cyrene stepped in, like Mary did watching her Son suffer and die. We will fret and worry about the things we have no control over, but we can take a different perspective on our suffering. It is possible to suffer gracefully (full of grace). Our suffering can be redemptive.

While on my Cursillo weekend, I learned the meaning of the word *palanca*. Palanca is the Spanish word for "lever" and it is a form of prayer where we leverage our physical suffering for a redemptive purpose. This is not a new concept, as the Catholic Church has always encouraged mortification as a way to make sacrifices for the sake of others.

We can make these small sacrifices, for example, by offering up our prayers for others, or going without for the good of another in fasting. I personally give up sleep for more prayer time because sleep is precious to me. "For if you live according to the flesh you will die, but if by the Spirit you put to death the deeds of the body you will live" (Rom. 8:13).

By practicing palanca, or mortification, our sacrifices can be used for the good of another. In our death to self, we allow our sin to be put to rest. St. John Climacus said it this way: "Humility is the only thing that no devil can imitate."

Aligning myself with Mary through my sufferings showed me that God is offering all of Himself to love me through this. But what

I witnessed through Mary is her faithfulness and trust in the message the angel Gabriel delivered.

I still sometimes fight against feelings of unworthiness. This usually comes about when I think I'm not qualified for something or when I feel like I should know more. I read what I write, I look at myself in pictures of ministry at church, and I ask God *Who is this? Who is this woman who has been healed?* Sometimes I don't recognize her, because I know what I've been through and it just seems surreal. In humility, I have come to see myself again as a beautiful woman of the Lord.

God holds close those who have suffered the most. He promised He would. He gives us graces that only we can understand, and we know that these graces are to be valued and held on to. Those who feel too weak or who struggle to feel His strength, He empowers to say yes.

It's not just trust and faith that we have for ourselves, but it's the same trust we have when we empower others to do great things, in the name of Jesus. We unite ourselves to those who are in need of Jesus, and we ask God to magnify it to His Glory. We say yes for their souls, for the sake of their rest. We help them rest in Him.

When we do this in His name, we are blessed indeed. It has nothing to do with us, but everything to do with God. We use the gifts He has given us to make a difference, not only in our own life, but also in our family's life, and in the lives of the people we surround ourselves with.

May our yes to God's gifts—His blessings, His healing, His sacrifices, His everything—be a resounding yes like Mary's, where we choose to be faithful and follow Christ. It's a decision He has given us to make—accept His desire to love you through this loss.

I realized on that retreat weekend that my journey toward complete healing always needed to be made alongside Our Lady, walking toward her Son's Sacred Heart. I felt her desire to help me to love her Son the way she does and to always strive to keep the Incarnation alive. I left the retreat with a light and beautiful heart filled with so many things to ponder and keep inside.

Grieving parents, hear me. We represent Mary. If you have entered into this role as a parent who has lost a child and you aren't clinging to Mary for guidance and understanding, you are missing out on a lifetime of help, peace, and grace.

We look to Mary to be a role model because her mission became protecting Christ's legacy, His mission, and His Church. And through her demonstration of perfect discipleship, we have a role model to try and live up to.

I am not worthy to ever say I walked in Mary's shoes, because her feet crushed the serpent's head. Mary was the instrument that God chose to defeat death. Her womb birthed Christ so that we could spend eternity with Him in heaven; and when Mary said yes to God, she demonstrated pure obedience to Christ.

Obedience is something I struggle with daily. I was barely strong enough to echo a whispered yes compared to her profound, confident yes. My prayer is that Mary, Mother of God, will teach me how to trust fully, to serve faithfully, to be totally obedient. I know nothing of this, so she must teach me her ways.

My understanding of the passion, resurrection, and Ascension came with deep suffering, but I found healing at the foot of the cross. Finally, I realized after seven years of suffering through my grief, that when I was healed, Jesus led me to the other side of the cross. He resurrected me, liberated me, and transformed me, making broken look beautiful.

I hope that through this book, no matter what stage of grief you are in, that you will find some peace and understanding of just how much our Good Father loves you, and He desires to bring you to the other side of the resurrection as well.

Chapter Twenty-One

WHAT DOES MARRIAGE LOOK LIKE FOR BEREAVED COUPLES?

"Greater love has no man than this, that a man lay down his life for his friends . . . You did not choose me, but I chose you and appointed you that you should go and bear fruit and that your fruit should abide; so that whatever you ask the Father in my name, he may give it to you."

—John 15:13, 16

MANY PEOPLE ARE UNSURE WHAT TO DO FOR A GRIEVing parent.

The word *compassion* in Latin means "co-suffering." Compassion involves "feeling for another" and is a precursor to empathy. But *empathy* (to suffer with) is a function of the virtue of charity by which a person enters into another's feelings, needs, and suffering. No matter what that person is going through, we show Christ to them by having compassion and entering into empathy with them. That is how we can help the grieving parent, and that is how we can love them through this.

Everyone grieves differently and for different lengths of time. It may take someone a year, it may take seven years, a decade, or a lifetime; but don't ever assume that the griever's hurt is gone. We can still exist with our wounds, like Christ did in the Upper Room after His resurrection. But out of the person's suffering, we can offer charity. Many people who suffer do so in private, behind closed doors. I cried at night in bed while my husband wiped my tears and held me. Not many people witnessed my deep, scourging pain, but Ryan did, and Ryan just kept loving me through the tears.

Our grief created this unwanted, invisible wedge in our marriage that we couldn't figure out how to get rid of. Some of our reactions were in line with how couples were supposed to grieve and some should never have happened—those came out of our hurt. I threw verbal darts at him like we were in target practice; each one aimed at the bull's eye.

We didn't know where to find help. Issues arose that we could not fix ourselves. We had experienced the very the same loss, but were grieving in drastically different ways. I wanted Him to be my safety net, but he didn't understand what was going on inside of me.

I found myself not being able to focus on Ryan's needs because I could barely take care of myself. I felt a profound sense of isolation and focused on stabilizing my feelings, which took everything I had. I didn't have time or energy to process how Ryan must have been feeling. I was very selfish with my emotions.

Our marriage suffered for a long time. Sometimes, emotions of resentment, anger, hurt, or abandonment would bubble up out of the haze. At times I felt unloved by my husband—a feeling he never intended, but because we were not communicating about our grief, and because we didn't know how to work through the obstacles, our marriage grew stagnant.

We needed to be talking to each other. We should have gone to therapy, but pride blinded us. We thought we could survive this on our own. We hadn't invited God into the equation. We were wrong in almost every aspect of handling our grief, but we didn't know better. We didn't know a "right way." We felt like we had no resources.

I took a passive approach; I was just waiting for the pain to go away. I kept telling myself, in time, life would go back to normal. I did not have a full understanding of the grieving process, so the tornado of emotions came and left destruction in its wake.

After some time, I understood that I was too blinded by my grief to properly identify what was going inside my heart. I couldn't name the emotions that kept resurfacing. Because of my inability to identify what they were, I determined I wouldn't be able to fix them.

I still don't quite understand how our marriage survived when we were both in that black hole. By the grace of God, there was never a time that we looked at each other and thought we had gone through too much to recover from. We never got to a place when we thought the easier choice would be to just give up. Thankfully, we are both stubborn and refuse to become a statistic of divorce due to child loss. This relentlessness was what carried us through those valleys.

In acknowledging the immense amount of suffering and pain we endured, it became clear to both of us that this was the reason we continued to hold on. We had been through a lifetime of sadness, hurt, anger, and a storm of emotions that most couples never experience. There we stood, just as clueless of what was going on inside our hearts as on the day we met. But this time was different, the love that remained was the same. The love never left. We just needed to find each other again through the mess of our grief.

Time and time again, God extended grace to us that we did not deserve but desperately needed in order to withstand this tragedy. We had so many reasons to end our marriage. Reasons that were the direct result of the grief, but love kept us together. We loved each other so much, and God took our love and let it become another piece to our healing.

In our work with grieving couples, we've noticed mothers and fathers almost always grieve differently. While the mother's grief is often visible, the father's grief may be internalized. One parent may become angry or lash out at someone or something. One parent may resent God, and the other may trust fully. One parent may stop going to church, and one may start attending more often. One parent may cry all day, every day, and one may not cry at all in front of people— even their spouse.

My grief was agonizing and remained that way for a period of around seven years. I cried all of the time, and so I spent a lot of time alone at home. Ryan was very private about his grief and did not show his emotions openly, even to me. The magnitude of this invisible wedge in our marriage was intense.

I am truly blessed to have the small family that I have, and I thank God every day for sending me the support of my spiritual sisters to make it through each day. They help me be a better person, they challenge me to become holier than the day before, and they lift me up when I feel like I've failed. This is my support system, a family of friends who chose to walk this journey with one another, growing closer to Christ.

You see, without each one of these beautiful friends, Ryan and I would be going through this life together, but on our own. Having a community of fellow travelers walking with us makes the hard times bearable. It is important to have friends with the same high ideals: friends who want to get to heaven and to grow their families in holiness. Families who want to have good clean fun. And, boy, do we have a lot of fun.

I've come to realize what an incredible gift of a husband I have. I didn't always think of him this way, and it pains my heart to admit this. His gentle touch to wipe my tears was the most beautiful sight that anyone would ever witness, and I had the privilege of receiving this incredible deed. I'm ashamed to say I did not thank him for each time he did this. John 15:13 explains this kind of love. "Greater love has no man than this, that a man lay down his life for his friends." This verse is how Ryan loves me. This verse is how much Jesus loves me. Enough to lay His life down for me.

Fr. McIntyre expressed this in a beautiful way:

> To love without ceasing, loving all the way to heaven, that is what marriage is all about, and to desire the good for the other.
>
> Marriage is the closest and most intimate of

human friendships. It involves the sharing of the whole of a person's life with his/her spouse. Marriage calls for a mutual self-surrender so intimate and complete that spouses—without losing their individuality—become "one," not only in body, but in soul.

The four things that love has to be are:

1. Free
2. Total (unconditional, complete)
3. Faithful
4. Fruitful

God commanded us to love, but with our free wills we are given the choice to love. Choose Love.

God doesn't force us to love, it is an invitation. We should love our spouses and each other in the same way that Jesus loves us. Jesus served the friends He loved by washing their feet. There are many instances in Scripture where Jesus is both master/servant, victim/sacrifice, lion/lamb. We should love freely with humility, and help our spouses rise up in truth and love.

Have you ever stopped to ask your spouse how you can help them get to heaven? This question hit me hard when I read it at a marriage retreat we attended during lent one year. I had never considered this before. The power in each spouse answering this simple question will transform your marriage. Our sole desire had been to see Emma Grace and Talon in heaven, but we had not been talking about getting each other there.

For a while, I only wanted to get to heaven to see the twins. I wasn't so much desiring to be by God, the One I was angry with. Through our marriage, I've been given a small taste of heaven by the incredible gift that Ryan is to me. He redefined what love looks and feels like. I desire holiness and to one day worship with him the eternal God. We hope to do this as a whole family. I want to see my twins again.

Transforming your marriage will take longer than one season. Our faith journey transformed our marriage. The more we learned about what God designed marriage to be, and understood the sacrament of marriage, the closer we were able to enter into this profound love that is only possible through the grace of God.

This full understanding of marriage came at a high price. We had to accept and trust that the difficulties, dangers, and even deaths of our children allowed us the opportunity to grow in these virtues we lacked. I know that God did not take Talon and Emma so that we could become better people, or a better couple, but through our grief, He gave us the gift of transformation; so that we were able to also grow in love with Christ and each other. We believe that what our love created, our love had to heal. We must keep that communion with Christ to keep that communion with our spouse, because ultimately, our spouse reveals to us how much we are loved by Christ.

Here are a few ways you can show great acts of love to your spouse:

- Help with the chores.
- Stop to pray with your spouse when you see hurt on his/her face.

- Leave work early when you know he/she is having a bad day.
- Reorder your loves. First is our love of God, then our love of our spouse in communion with Christ, and then our love of our children in communion with Christ. When you reorder your priorities, you will find peace within yourself.

I desire for you to feel the love of Christ through your spouse. It starts with a small step. Decide today to pray for and with your spouse for your mutual healing.

Chapter Twenty-Two

YOUR HEALING PLAN

"The hardest thing I've ever had to do was watch my children die, and the second hardest thing I've had to do was live every day since those two moments."

—Anonymous

WHERE DO WE GO FROM HERE?

I wish there was one answer that I could give you, but unfortunately this ministry is so personal and relational that I would be remiss to say your healing will occur in a day, a month, or a year. More than likely, it will take a lifetime.

I say a lifetime because one day when we face the Lord in glory in heaven, only then will there be no more pain. That's when our kingdom will have no end, and the joy of our hearts will reside with Jesus and with our children.

But we all know that for us to be in line to enter the gates of heaven, we have work to do here on earth to begin our conversion, reversion, the deepening of our faith.

I've put together a step-by-step guide that helped me in my journey of processing my grief and beginning the healing process. I pray it will be a starting point for you.

1. **Examination of Conscience:** Do a deep examination of conscience so you can be raw and real with your confessor. Jesus is waiting patiently for you to invite Him into your suffering. Let Him extend His mercy upon you. If you've never done an examination of conscience before, I recommend you visit the USCCB.org website: www.usccb.org/prayer-and-worship/sacramentsandsac-ramentals/penance/examinations-of-conscience.cfm

2. **Confession:** Make an appointment with your priest for Confession. I prefer to do this face-to-face, but some people are more comfortable behind a screen. The point is to go, so do what you're most comfortable with. Trust me, you won't regret this. Jesus pours graces onto us by celebrating this sacrament. Don't leave these graces unclaimed!

3. **Mass:** Make sure you attend Mass every Sunday and on Holy Days of Obligation. If you aren't registered in a parish, visit the Catholic Churches in your area and decide where you want to become a member. Being part of a family and having a priest who is praying for you and your family is very important to your soul and your faith. Community and relationships are super important and are what builds our kingdom.

4. **Pray with your family:** Every day and every night. If

you want to learn more about a person, pray with them. This is where you hear their heart out loud. Praying together is the single most important example you can set for your children. There are many ways to pray as a family. We use the Faith5 method[22] or you can take turns reciting the following prayers: the Our Father, Hail Mary, Glory Be, the prayer to St. Michael the Archangel, the Memorare, and the Hail Holy Queen. Before each prayer, a person can offer up their special intentions or prayer request. This takes about ten minutes. At our house, we end by asking for our favorites saint's intercession. This sets the stage to end the day with a peaceful heart.

5. **Find a spiritual director:** You can get spiritual direction as a couple or individually. After prayerful consideration, ask a priest, deacon, religious, or layperson that is certified if they can provide you with ongoing spiritual direction. Spiritual directors should not charge you for spiritual direction under any circumstance. For a good book on spiritual direction, check out: *Navigating the Interior Life* by Daniel Burke.

6. **Counseling:** If you need counseling, consider going to a counselor who is Catholic. It is important for you to see someone who shares the same faith and morals as you. A counselor who is coming from a different worldview can lead you down a variant path at a time when

---

[22] For more information on this method, visit http://www.faith5.org/

you are most vulnerable. This could be detrimental to your mental health and possibly to your salvation.

7. **Find a support group:** Start by contacting your parish office or diocese to see what grief support groups are offered in your area. Be prepared to hear the words, "We don't have anything available." This was my experience. It is what lit the flame to even consider starting a support group within our diocese. Many parishes have established support groups, though, so ask to see what's available. You can also continue to check our website www.redbird.love as our educational and programs grow and evolve.

8. **Make a friend:** As hard as this may sound, reach out to your priest to see if there are other parents in your parish who are suffering from child loss, even if it's been some time ago. Just talking with another couple can release so much pent-up pain. If there is no one within your parish, reach out through social media. Child loss is not often talked about openly, but when you meet someone who has experienced the same kind of loss, it's like encountering an old friend you've never met. Having a friend who has gone through this is priceless. We can love each other through our losses. Let people love you! Ask your new friend to mentor you through the program. This will provide healing for both of you.

9. **Start your own group:** We started Red Bird with the intention of ministering to families who have experienced child loss. Consider starting a small faith-sharing

group for people who have lost a loved one. Ask your priest if you can advertise something in your weekly bulletin. Don't be afraid to say, "Hey, I'm hurting. I need help, and I want to help you too." Come up with some guidelines for how the sessions will run, such as:

- Give everyone a chance to share.
- Don't feel like you have to offer the grieving person advice; sometimes they just need someone to listen.
- Stick to the allotted time, whatever you decide that will be (one hour, etc.).
- Begin and end each session with prayer.

The only sure way to fail is to do nothing. As we say in Cursillo, "Find a friend, be a friend, and bring your friend to Christ."

10. **Attend a Cursillo Weekend:** You deserve a weekend away to learn more about your faith and to grow deeper in your relationship with Jesus. This was by far the best thing that I did for my family and myself. Cursillo is a three-day walk with the Holy Spirit where you listen to clergy and laypeople give talks about the Catholic faith. I received so much healing and graces during my Cursillo weekend, my cup was overflowing for the first time in a long time. And it's a great way to form new friendships.

11. **Join a Bible study:** Studying the Bible is crucial to learning more about your faith. Our faith is rich and extensive. By studying the Bible, you educate yourself

on why the Church believes as it does. Knowing more about Jesus by reading Scripture will enrich your faith life in innumerable ways. For instance, when I read and contemplated the passion of Christ from the perspective of each of the four Gospel accounts, I saw Christ's sacrifice as so much more than just words on a page. It helped me to define in a tangible way what compassion and empathy actually looked like.

12. **Teach your kids about Jesus and what He did for us on the cross:** We can only protect the faith by teaching our children about Christ. If you feel called to teach religious education, this is another incredible way to give back to the Church. There is much work to do and not enough workers. Volunteer and form a personal relationship with your priest and church family. In most instances, no experience is required. It is crucial that we pass on the faith to our young people.

More than anything else you can do in your healing journey, participating in the sacraments is the most important. In addition to attending Mass every Sunday with your family, invite family members who are irregular attendees. If you ever skip Mass for a reason other than illness, it is appropriate to go to Reconciliation before taking communion again.

I've gotten great solace from spending time in the Adoration chapel when I'm especially blue. Bring your suffering to unite with His suffering, cry it out in the chapel where Jesus is present in the tabernacle. If you don't have an Adoration chapel in your church, check nearby parishes, or have an honest conversation with your priest about your grieving and tell him what a comfort it would be to just go sit in church. He may give you a code to get in and adore Christ all by yourself in the sanctuary.

If you haven't finished your sacraments, don't delay. Don't take the gifts that Christ is offering for granted. Join RCIA and make an honest effort to complete the sacraments that are available to you.

One day, we will look back on our life, and we will be able to pinpoint a pivotal moment when we knew something changed. That moment when we looked and felt different because something inside was different. We will talk differently, dress differently, our schedules will change, as will how we spend our money. And for the first time, we may be able to accept our children's deaths and be excited to talk to them about what heaven is like. This may come out of left field one day, surprise you, and shake you to the core.

A line will be drawn in the sand delineating your life before and after. For some, it will be glorious, and for others, it will be a balance on a fine line. But one thing is certain, we will never feel this freedom, nor will we ever experience a radical transformation, if we do not experience the love of the Father first.

My life finally makes sense looking back. I can see all of the times that Jesus moved me out of harm's way. I can see all the doors He closed, and all the doors He opened. I can see the people He brought into my life, and the ones He took away. I can see the career paths He chose for me, and those He quietly cast away.

There were many times I blamed Jesus for breaking my heart, but He wasn't breaking it to do me harm; He was breaking it to transform and transfix me. Trust the way Jesus is transforming you.

Surrender to His pruning. Embrace the graces that He gives to you when you choose to follow Him radically. I have given Christ countless reasons not to love me, none of them changed His mind.

As St. Francis of Assisi said, "Start by doing what is necessary; then do what's possible, and suddenly you will be doing the impossible."

DEAR GRIEVING MOMS AND DADS,

Let Him enter into your suffering because, the good Father that He is, He will hold you as long as you need Him to, and if you fall again, you can run back into His arms again and again. Cry it out, scream, but do not ever stop loving Christ, because He is the only one who can remove the dark from your heart, pick up the million pieces, and beautifully piece it back together again.

Jesus is the only heart maker, the only heart restorer, the only heart purifier; He is the Sacred Heart. He is Divine Love. Allow Jesus to mend your heart back together. Allow Him to pick you up when you fall, allow Him to be the Savior of your heart. Allow Him to do this, every time, always, and forever.

This is my prayer for you.

Kelly

RECOMMENDED RESOURCES

Books:

The Catechism of the Catholic Church

Diary of Saint Maria Faustina Kowalska: Divine Mercy in My Soul
Walking with Mary by Edward Sri
Story of a Soul by St. Thérèse of Lisieux
Heaven Is for Real by Todd Burpo and Lynn Vincent (also on DVD)
Navigating the Interior Life by Daniel Burke

Movies:

Pope John Paul II
The Letters
Faustina, the Apostle of Divine Mercy

ACKNOWLEDGMENTS

Ryan, through the last two decades, you have been my saving grace. You have redefined what love looks like to me. You have given me so much love and mercy. At times I did not deserve it. As our hearts were broken from losing Talon, Emma Grace, and Christian, you have held me in your strong arms and shown me the face of Christ. Thank you for being such a beacon of light to me in my darkness. I will love you forever.

Estelle, my little shining star, your bubbly and vivacious personality is so contagious. Your attention to others' suffering has always been the most beautiful part of your heart. Thank you for always being attentive to my tears. But mostly, for all the times you saw me cry and wrapped your little arms around me and kissed my cheeks. When the weight of my grief was so heavy, even though you were scared, you didn't leave me. You always made me smile through my tears.

My three little saints, because of you, I now know who Jesus is. Thank you for paving a golden path to heaven for us. Please continue to serve the Lord and intercede for us when you see our hearts pained with sorrow. And walk with Our Lady as she gathers her little saints in heaven. Pray for us until we meet again.

Jesus, You are the one I need to thank the most. By becoming human and dying on the cross, You conquered death. You have given me the hope for heaven. Thank You for loving me, a beloved daughter of the Mighty King. I now understand my worth and the gifts You have given me to glorify Your kingdom. I finally learned how to wear my holy crown—the crown of love and mercy You crafted exclusively for me.

I only wish to be more like You as You spent Your entire ministry focusing on the sinners and brokenhearted. Please allow me to continue to serve those who are directly in front of me who are dying a spiritual death from grief. I promise not to focus on the numbers we serve, but the person we are serving. Please help me to navigate the imprint of pain in their hearts by opening mine to authentically serve and love them exactly how they need to be served and loved. I love You, Jesus. Have mercy on us.

Fr. McIntyre, you will never know how much you helped me in those most vulnerable moments in Confession, when you allowed God to use you to speak truth to my darkness. For this and every other time you supported Ryan and me in our journey to holiness, thank you. I pray every day that God will bless your vocation and for you to remain a holy and compassionate priest. Thank you for the gift of your vocation to our family.

Courtney, thank you for pushing me to say yes to this ministry when

I was so scared of opening my wounds and being vulnerable with others. You are one of my forty. I hope you know that you will always be one of my favorite creative minds. I love you.

To Misty and Ashley, thank you both for always challenging me to go deeper with God and for supporting me through my conversion. I love you two so much and pray that God blesses our efforts to love Him great.

To Brittany, thank you for always being the smiling face in my darkness. When words failed, you loved me anyway. I didn't need to know what you were thinking because your heart was saying it all. I love you and pray for your family every day.

To my sister, thank you for loving me despite all the darts I threw your way. Thank you for loving me when I was in intense darkness and wasn't really lovable. You saw the side of me that I hid from most people and instead of running, you stayed. You stayed by my side and tried to help even when you had no idea how to. You stayed even though you were scared out of your mind that your sister had changed. Thank you for having courage enough to not give up on me. I love and pray for you daily to always find the peace and joy that you desire, because you deserve it. I love you so much.

And the many, many people who touched my life and helped put a smile on my face when all I wanted to do was lay in my bed and cry. Thank you all for trying your hardest to understand what I was going through and loving me despite my darkness. Your love and kindness did not go unnoticed. Thanks to the city of Breaux Bridge for keeping our community safe and making it a beautiful place to raise our families. Thank you, to all of the parishioners of St. Bernard Catholic Church, for welcoming our family back to church when we needed to belong and be loved. Thank you to our friends, those who stuck around through the hard parts of our life. Lastly, to our entire family for sitting with us through the tears and pain, in the darkest parts of our journey. We love you for trying to help us in the best way you could.

"I shall love you. I shall love you always: when day breaks, when evening turns into night, at every hour, at every moment. I shall love you always, always, always."

—St. Gemma Galgani

RED BIRD MINISTRIES

IS A CATHOLIC GRIEF-SUPPORT
NON-PROFIT MINISTRY SERVING
INDIVIDUALS AND COUPLES WHO HAVE
LOST SOMEONE THEY LOVE, WITH
SPECIAL ATTENTION FOR THOSE WHO
HAVE EXPERIENCED THE LOSS OF A
CHILD FROM PREGNANCY THROUGH
ADULTHOOD, AND THOSE WHO HAVE
LOST A SPOUSE OR PARENT.

www.redbird.love

Engagement, summer of 2002

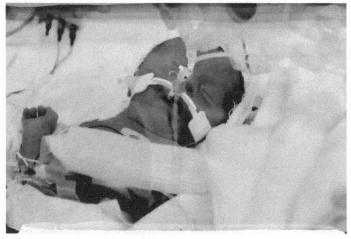

Talon Antoine, NICU, October 2005

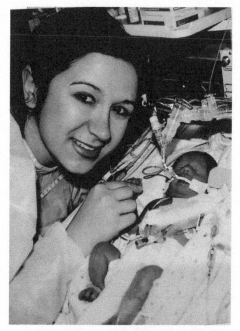

Talon Antoine, NICU, October 2005

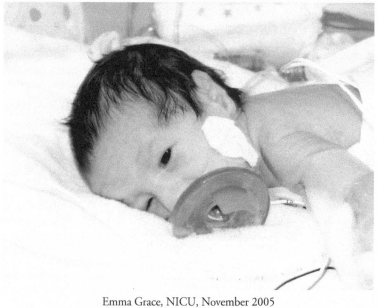

Emma Grace, NICU, November 2005

Emma Grace's Baptism, September 10, 2005

Emma Grace, Easter 2007

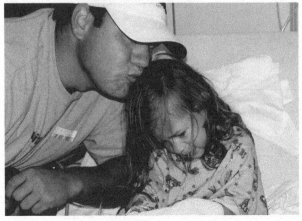

Emma Grace, Children's Hospital CT Scan, 2008

Emma Grace, Women's and Children's Hospital, Rotavirus, 2008

Emma Grace and Dad, dinner, 2008

Emma Grace and Estelle, May 2009

Emma Grace, June 2009

Emma Grace, June 2009

Emma Grace and Estelle, June 2009

Emma Grace, July 2009

Emma Grace and Mom, July 2009

Disney, July 2009

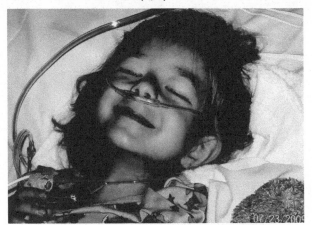

Emma Grace, diagnosed with H1N1, July 2009

Emma Grace's funeral, September 16, 2009

Family photo, 2017

15-year Anniversary Blessing, July 15, 2017